I0760125

A GUIDE TO HILLFORTS of BRITAIN AN AERIAL VIEW

A GUIDE TO HILLFORTS of BRITAIN AN AERIAL VIEW

THE LEGACY OF THE IRON AGE DOBUNNI TRIBE

NICHOLAS SHARPE

Pen & Sword
MILITARY

Published in Great Britain in 2025 by
PEN & SWORD MILITARY
An imprint of
Pen & Sword Books Ltd
Yorkshire - Philadelphia

ISBN 978 1 03611 5 531

A CIP catalogue record for this book is available from the British Library

Book Design by Dominic Allen

Pen & Sword Books Limited incorporates the imprints of Atlas, Archaeology, Aviation, Discovery, Family History, Fiction, History, Maritime, Military, Military Classics, Politics, Select, Transport, True Crime, Air World, Frontline Publishing, Leo Cooper, Remember When, Seaforth Publishing, The Praetorian Press, Wharncliffe Local History, Wharncliffe Transport, Wharncliffe True Crime & White Owl.

For a complete list of Pen & Sword titles please contact:
PEN & SWORD BOOKS LIMITED
47 Church Street, Barnsley, South Yorkshire, S70 2AS, England
E-mail: enquiries@pen-and-sword.co.uk
Website: www.pen-and-sword.co.uk
Or
PEN AND SWORD BOOKS
1950 Lawrence Rd, Havertown, PA 19083, USA
E-mail: Uspen-and-sword@casematepublishers.com
Website: www.penandswordbooks.com

CONTENTS

INTRODUCTION

There are a significant number of Iron Age hillforts on the edge of the limestone scarp of the western boundary of the Cotswold Hills, stretching north to south through the length of Gloucestershire. This is the area where I grew up and still reside, and they have held a certain fascination for me since I was a young child. Family walks would quite often entail a visit to one of these sites, and still one of my favourite dog walks is to take in a circuit of my local hillfort, Uley Bury, with its commanding views of the Severn Vale below, extending down to the Severn Bridge, the Bristol Channel and South Wales beyond. Over several years, my visits, photography and research of hillforts has extended all over the West Country, including Somerset, Wiltshire, Oxfordshire, Gloucestershire and Hampshire, up to Herefordshire, Worcestershire and Shropshire. Aware that the area occupied by modern-day Gloucestershire was the centre of the Iron Age Dobunni tribe, my research became increasingly focused on this tribe's sphere of influence as it extended into neighbouring counties. Using information and research from eminent historians and archaeologists in the field of the Iron Age period, though I am merely an enthusiastic local historian, I have put forwards suggestions to build a picture of the borders of the Dobunnic tribal region by using the location of hillforts and geographic factors, including rivers, marshes and hill ranges.

The aim of the book is to explain to the reader and give a background knowledge of what a hillfort is, including its construction, development and different classifications, using aerial drone photography to illustrate the subject. Then questions are asked: Who were the Dobunni tribe? When were these structures built? What was their known history and what was their relationship with the land, particularly to these ancient earthworks? Hopefully after answering these questions, the reader will be armed with the relevant information so that when physically visiting these sites, instead of looking at what the layman would say are just banks of turf, the earthworks can be fully appreciated and the visitor will have an understanding of who our ancient ancestors were and the structures they built which remain with us today. With the advent and wide use of drone photography nowadays, a whole new perspective of these fascinating earthworks opens up to the viewer. After looking at these aerial images, hopefully the reader will be inspired to put his or her walking boots on and visit some of these spectacular sites. On any visit to a hillfort, I love to walk the ramparts and take in the scale of the construction to appreciate and gain a feel for the area and its geographic position.

From my visits to these locations, I have included information on where to park using what3words, the length of the walk and its difficulty, mainly gradient, on a scale of one to four (four being the hardest). The list of specific hillforts I discuss in this book is not exhaustive; there are many others located in the area discussed in this book. However, I hope I have gathered together, especially for the reader and the prospective visitor, the most spectacular and still-intact collection of Iron Age earthworks. An invaluable aid I have found when out on the ground discovering these sites is the Ordnance Survey smartphone app. From showing footpaths and ancient monuments to planning your walk and plotting where you are on the ground at any time, it is a fantastic tool.

HILLFORTS: AN OVERVIEW

PREHISTORY TIMELINE

NEOLITHIC 4000–2500 BC

BRONZE AGE 2500–700 BC

IRON AGE 700 BC–43 AD

ROMAN INVASION AND OCCUPATION 43–410 AD

'A hillfort is a type of earthworks used as a fortified refuge or defended settlement, located to exploit a rise in elevation for a defensive advantage.' This is an often-used quote to describe a hillfort, but it is a general one; as we will find out, not all were necessarily sited on elevated land and the term 'defended enclosure' may be a more suitable one to describe many of the sites discussed here. However, the term 'hillfort' will be used as the generic name for the subject matter of this book.

'As early as the Neolithic period about 3000 BC a few hilltops were being fortified in a manner that might constitute the beginnings of hillforts.' (James Dyer, 2003). Crickley Hill, Gloucestershire (page 65), a site of international archaeological importance has evidence of occupation dating back to at least 3700 BC as a Neolithic 'causewayed enclosure'.

A 'causewayed enclosure' is a type of large prehistoric earthwork common to the early Neolithic in Europe, marked out by ditches and banks, with a number of causeways crossing the ditches. Evidence suggests that the enclosures were visited on occasion by the Neolithic people rather than being a site of permanent occupation. Archaeological excavations have discovered human remains, pottery and animal bones in the banks and ditches of the enclosures; this has been seen as an attempt by the people visiting and rebuilding the site to connect with their ancestors and have a religious monument to signify their attachment to that area with repeated rituals. Back in the Neolithic period when these enclosures were constructed, archaeology suggests that Europe, including Britain, was heavily forested and the enclosures were rare clearings used for occasional rituals, feasting and celebrations on certain dates of their ancient calendar.

Windmill Hill is a classic example of a Neolithic 'causewayed enclosure' with three concentric but intermittent ditches. It is part of the Avebury World Heritage site in Wiltshire.

For the next 2000 years, there seems little sign of fortifications being built. Settlements at this time would have been modest defended enclosures that would have consisted of a small number of roundhouses, stock pens and granaries surrounded by a wooden palisade with perhaps a defensive ditch. These enclosures may have been built for a variety of reasons: protection of livestock from natural predators, preventing neighbouring communities stealing stock and providing a basic defensive structure for the settlement.

From the late Bronze Age through to the Iron Age, approximately 1300-100 BC, earthwork enclosures were being constructed all over Britain and Ireland. According to the 2017 Atlas of Hillforts of Britain and Ireland, an extensive piece of work carried out by Oxford University, there are 4147 of these sites dotted over the British Isles and Ireland.

Towards the end of the second millennium BC, during the middle Bronze Age, a number of hilltops appear to have been protected with ramparts, ditches and sometimes wooden palisades. What had changed in society to warrant the building of these defences? A major reason from recent studies suggests that from 1000 BC, the climate in Britain began to deteriorate from the relative warmth of the early Bronze Age. This meant that by the Iron Age, the climate was very much as we experience it today. From a scientific study of Scottish midge larvae, where in a warmer climate they would be abundant, from 800 BC there appears a significant increase in cold-water species and a marked decrease in warm-water species, such as the midge larvae. This occurred over a relatively short period of time, about 50 years or so. This corresponds with other evidence from pollen and peat bogs which indicate that as the temperature declined, rainfall increased. This would have been a matter of life and death for Iron Age communities, as too much sun will wither a crop, but too much rain means a crop will not ripen and the result is no harvest. Upland areas that were farmed in the Bronze Age were no longer productive agricultural land. It is believed that this resulted in increased competition for the well-drained lowland areas for farming, leading to increased tension, perhaps increased aggression and ultimately conflict between communities. Defence and territory became increasingly important factors in these hostile times. As a result, defended hilltop settlements developed: 'The ultimate defensive weapon of European prehistory was the hillfort of the first millennium BC' (Michael Avery, 1986).

Communities in Britain during the Bronze and Iron Age were organized in tribal groups, each ruled by a local chieftain. Many archaeologists regard hillforts as symbols of wealth and power, with local chieftains using these structures to assert their influence over the local area. As these communities evolved, early interactions with each other seem to have been confrontational, perhaps as tribal groups and their boundaries settled into place. This inter-tribal warfare was traditionally interpreted as the reason for building hillforts: defensive areas where communities across the region could muster and have somewhere to stand their ground when threatened.

Sometime after the eighth century BC and for the next 200 years, two different types of fortification were constructed in Southern Britain. Firstly, large hilltop enclosures were established, often between 6–20 ha in area. The defences were fairly weak, consisting of a timber-faced rampart or drystone wall with an outer shallow, flat-bottomed ditch. From excavations of sites of this size, there seems an apparent absence of internal occupation on any scale, and with the relatively simple nature of the defences and gates, this might suggest that these structures were built primarily for the collection and protection of cattle. An example of this would be Bathampton Down enclosure near Bath, north-east Somerset, covering 80 acres, but also located close to pastureland in the valley of the river Avon.

Secondly, fortified enclosures appear, strongly defended with timber or stone and sited on prominent ridges and spurs/promontories ranging in size from 2–4ha. These usually show signs of occupation over a long period, with occasional strengthening and extensions of the fortified circuit. An example would be found at Croft Ambrey hillfort in Herefordshire, where the structure experienced seven phases of occupation between 450 BC and 49 AD, and where the initial footprint was 3.6ha, but with two further banks and ditches constructed, was increased to enclose 8.4ha.

The major period of hillfort construction occurred between the sixth and early fourth centuries BC. Contour and plateau (level terrain) forts of around 5ha in area appear in many parts of southern England again, with timber faced or stone ramparts and now V-shaped ditches. 'By the fourth century BC emerge a number of dominant developed hillforts, each extremely well defended with multiple lines of banks and ditches' (James Dyer, 2003). These large hillfort enclosures may be regarded as regional capitals, permanently occupied and used as important political, social and religious centres. There was also industry, with metal and leather working and trade with markets to sell the finished goods, as well as livestock and food stuffs. So, looking at the Dobunnic tribal area of the West Country, the 'regional capitals' could include the oppida at Bagendon, Gloucestershire, as well as the large, major hillfort locations of British Camp in the Malvern Hills and also in Herefordshire, Credenhill Camp comprising the third largest hillfort earthworks in Britain after Ham Hill, Somerset and Maiden Castle, Dorset.

DEVELOPMENT OF HILLFORT CONSTRUCTION

TIMBER PALISADES

'Whenever excavation has been adequate, palisades if they occur can be shown to precede earthwork defences' (Barry Cunliffe, 1974). Blewburton Hill, Oxfordshire, is an example of where a small timber palisaded settlement dates to around 550 BC. This was later replaced

Blewburton Hill from above, looking down on the original palisaded settlement on the summit of the hill and the later outer banks and ditches which extended the footprint of the fort.

in the fourth century BC by the first version of the hillfort, which covered twice the area as that included within the earlier palisade; this was enclosed with a single earthen rampart and shallow ditch.

Typical early palisade construction consisted of small or mid-sized tree trunks aligned vertically, with as little free space between them as possible, embedded in a continuous foundation trench without ditches or the banking up of soil behind. The most important consideration in construction was to provide a vertical wall of timber confronting the world outside. However, basic flaws remained; the timber would soon rot and would eventually have to be replaced. Timber could be easily fired by attackers, as archaeological evidence has shown at Crickley Hill, and Leckhampton Camp in Gloucestershire.

GLACIS OR DUMP-STYLE RAMPART

The associated problems of using timber were overcome by a new method of construction which appears to have been widely adopted in the south and east of Britain sometime in the fourth to the third century BC or after. Ditches were dug deeper and the rampart face was sheered back at an angle following the ditch side, thus creating

Croft Ambrey, Herefordshire, illustrating the use of glacis ramparts.

a continuous slope from the bottom of the ditch to the crest of the rampart at an angle of 30–45 degrees. Covered with loose scree and capped with a breastwork of timber or flint, the approach would have been daunting to any attacker. The only maintenance problem was to keep the ditch clear of silt. This would have been done periodically, the scree being thrown out on the downhill side, creating a spoil bank, sometimes referred to as a 'counterscarp'. In one section of Danebury Camp, Hampshire, it was possible to trace evidence of eleven different periods of addition to the counterscarp bank, each representing a periodic clearing-out operation.

This glacis (in military engineering terms, meaning an artificial slope) style of defences can be shown to replace timber structures at a number of sites. However, at Croft Ambrey, Herefordshire, dump

or glacis constructed ramparts and counterscarps were in use from the fifth or sixth century BC. There is evidence in southern Britain that dump ramparts were established by the sixth century BC in many locations.

Defending a site with a bank of soil and a ditch was long established, dating back into the second millennium. Examples include Welshbury Camp, Gloucestershire, dating to 1700 BC, and British Camp, Herefordshire, 1500 BC. Then, after a period when timber and stone-faced ramparts predominated, the older technique came back once more into common use and persisted until the Roman conquest.

TYPES OF HILLFORT

CONTOUR FORT

This is the most common type of fort, defined by the enclosing works approximately following a contour to retain roughly the same altitude around a hilltop. The chosen hill does not have to be particularly high to carry a contour fort. Maiden Castle (one of the largest hillforts in Britain) is an excellent example of a contour fort occupying a low elevation, only reaching a height of 25m above the surrounding land. Illustrated below is a fine example at Brent Knoll, Somerset.

PARTIAL CONTOUR FORT

A variant of the common contour fort is where one or more of the sectors enclosing circuit deviate radically from the chosen contour, generally to go down slope. An example is found at the complex site of Oldbury Castle, Wiltshire, photograph above, where the natural topography has dictated the layout of the fort which is not flat and varies up to 23m in height.

PROMONTORY HILLFORTS

These sites are set on promontories (i.e., between a river valley and that of an affluent), and in which the principal line or lines of enclosure are constructed across the easiest access. Manmade defensive earthworks may be absent on the sides, which are difficult to access, leaving these flanks to be protected by the natural fall of land such as the cliffs either side of Spital Meend fort, photograph above, and Symonds Yat fort, both located in Gloucestershire. These types of forts can be sited either on an inland promontory or sat on a coastal edge.

One of the only coastal promontory forts located in the Dobunnic tribal area is found at Wains Hill, Clevedon, Somerset. A single bank was built on the summit of a natural slope on the landward side of the promontory, running north to south. Parking available at St Andrews church (what3words: fingernails.trunk.those). The walk is 2.1 km, difficulty two. Landranger map 171. Map ref. NGR 390706.

Spital Meend promontory hillfort is sited on a spectacular west facing spur above a prominent bend and peninsula above the River Wye near Chepstow, Gloucestershire. The area of the fort is identified nowadays as the triangular field with the cliffs bounding the River Wye providing natural defence on the north- and south-facing sides. Ditches and ramparts were built across the landward side of the promontory and later seemingly incorporated into Offa's Dyke. The fort is located on private land with no public access; however, there is car parking opposite the location (what3words: interests.luring.early) and this is a good base to start a circular walk around the spectacular scenery of the peninsula to Lancaut and along the base of the cliffs of Wintour's Leap along the Wye. Landranger map 162. Map ref. NGR 542967.

HILLSLOPE FORT

This type of fort is defined by the entire circuit or circuits of the enclosing works being set on a hillslope, and not occupying either the hilltop or the valley bottom below the hill. An example, illustrated above is Knollbury Camp, Oxfordshire.

LEVEL TERRAIN (PLATEAU) FORT

This type of fort is defined by the entire circuit or circuits of the enclosing works being on level terrain, such that the immediate topography offers no dominant advantage due to altitude. For example, Segsbury Camp, Oxfordshire, occupying rolling countryside on the chalk escarpment, is located adjacent to the Ridgeway, an important ancient trackway that has been used for 5000 years and has been described as Britain's oldest road. The Ridgeway is seen in the photograph below in the upper left-hand corner, running east to west, parallel to Segsbury's southern bank and ditch.

Parking is off A338 in a lay-by on the Ridgeway heading east to White House Farm (what3words: homecare.cone.handbag). Cross the road; the walk heads west on the Ridgeway, with the fort located on the left; 3.2 km, difficulty one. Landranger map 174. Map ref. NGR 385845.

MARSH FORT

The marsh fort is defined by much of, if not the entire circuit of the enclosing earthworks, being set within a marshy area, usually by definition a fairly level area. For example, the Toots, Oldbury on Severn, Gloucestershire.

At the Toots, Oldbury on Severn, the circular shape of the fort is still visible from the remaining banks in the foreground, but much has been destroyed by development. This bivallate marsh fort occupies a slightly elevated position some 14m above sea level, which may originally have been a low-lying island in the Severn tidal salt marshes. Parking bays located opposite the Anchor Inn (what3words: nicknames.reverted.newsprint); a circular walk of 2.4km begins with a walk along the residential lane which skirts the outer bank and ditch, then the footpath bisects the earthworks from north to south via a local airfield; difficulty one.

DEFINITION OF HILLFORTS BY AREA

GREATER THAN 20HA

Keep in mind that 1ha = 10,000 sq. metres. Such hillforts are very large enclosures, meant to diffuse an area to defend, probably used for the protection of livestock. Various archaeologists operating in Britain have criticized the use of the term 'hillfort' both because of its perceived connection to fortifications and warfare and because not all such sites were actually located on hills. The late Professor of Archaeology Lesley Alcock believed that the term 'enclosed places' was more accurate, whilst British archaeologist J. Forde-Johnston commented on his preference for the term 'defensive enclosure'. These terms from eminent experts in this field do describe more accurately this size of earthwork.

An excellent example of a large enclosure is found at Bathampton Down near Bath, north-east Somerset. Occupying a flat limestone plateau standing at 204m above the valley of the River Avon to the north and east, this roughly rectangular univallate earthwork encloses an area of 32ha. With its slight defences comprising a single rampart with a flat-bottomed

ditch, there has been much debate concerning its use in the Iron Age period, with the consensus being that in all probability, the site was used as a stock enclosure. Bathampton Down is now predominantly a golf course, but a public footpath does follow the course of the earthworks, which are evident in places: just beware of flying golf balls. To the east, the steep slope, dropping down 170m to the River Avon, provided natural protection, but has been quarried for Bath Stone from the Roman era to the eighteenth century

The photograph above shows the extent of the enclosure, visible by the ring of trees on the summit; the bank and ditch are still evident within the tree line. On-street parking is available on Down Lane, Bathampton (what3words: supporter.silver.overnight). The footpath is opposite Down Lane across the A46 and leads straight up the hill. The walk is 3km; difficulty three/four. Landranger map 172. Map ref. NGR 774650.

1–20HA

These would be defended areas, large enough to support a permanent tribal settlement. An example illustrated above is Uley Bury, Gloucestershire.

SMALLER THAN 1HA

These are small enclosures, more likely to be individual farm homesteads or animal pens.

Blisbury Hill, Gloucestershire, is possibly a small Iron Age enclosed farmstead located on an isolated hillock with an elevation of 43m above the Severn Vale, which would have been surrounded on three sides by a tidal salt marsh.

RAMPARTS, WALLS AND DITCHES

When visiting the earthworks representing the visible remains of hillforts today, we see either grass-covered banks and U-shaped hollow ditches, or perhaps the tumbled walls of a stone-built fort. These earthworks can still be impressive with ramparts still standing 10m and more in height, as at Blaise Castle, Avon and Sutton Walls, Herefordshire. Often forts have survived best in woodland where

man has been unable to reduce the earthworks by ploughing and quarrying. This is true in remote areas where there has been no desire to remove the stone for more recent building purposes.

The inner rampart at Blaise Castle, Avon (previous page) is 10m high, and the same at Sutton Walls Hillfort, Herefordshire (above): both impressive defensive obstacles to any potential attacker. In both photographs, the footpaths are located within the inner ditch of the earthworks.

Within the classification of hillforts, there are three terms which further define the type of construction through the number of surrounding earthworks.

The impressive univallate hillfort of Liddington Castle, Wiltshire.

UNIVALLATE: A defended enclosure common in the later Bronze Age and Iron Age which is bounded by a single circuit of ramparts and ditches for enclosure and defence.

BIVALLATE: Where there is a double circuit of defensive earthworks and ditches.

The bivallate earthworks at Cadbury Camp, Tickenham, North Somerset.

MULTIVALLATE: Where there are three or more circuits of defensive earthworks. Confusingly nowadays the word multivallate is often applied to any fort with more than one line of defence. The outer works might not be complete circuits, but defend the weakest approaches. Typically, the inner circuit is original, with outer circuits added later.

Caer Caradoc, Chapel Lawn, Shropshire. Geographically this fort is located north of the River Teme, so would not have been a Dobunnic settlement. However, this is one of my favourite hillforts and is a fine example of multivallate earthworks. Parking is adjacent to the chapel in the village (what3words: marinated.reconnect.grazed); then a walk of 3.8km, initially via a track way, then a footpath which climbs up through ferns and scrub until the eastern entrance is outlined on the horizon above; difficulty four.

ENTRANCES

The point of greatest weakness in any fort was its entrance; even in the largest fort earthworks, the number of entrances was kept to a minimum. Entrances were particularly vulnerable to attack from battering and fire, and elaborate attempts were often made to make it increasingly difficult for attackers to reach the actual gates, by throwing up external earthworks or creating blind passages.

The simplest entrance consisted of a gap in the rampart and a corresponding causeway across any accompanying ditch. Sometimes no physical gate was present. A simple opening might indicate an enclosure for livestock rather than a defensive position. On a simple opening, the main ramparts may turn inwards or outwards, and be widened and heightened to control the entrance.

An example of a simple entrance is illustrated at the univallate earthworks at Liddington Castle, Wiltshire (above). This is a causewayed entrance built up with chalk rubble to cross the ditch and through the counterscarp, and then the main rampart, which possibly may have been faced with large chalk sarsen stones.

Written evidence of a simple entrance is mentioned in Julius Caesar's written memoirs of the invasion of Britain in 54 BC. Caesar writes of the attack on Bigbury hillfort, Kent, where he arrived at the head of the Legio

VII Claudia to find the site used as a stronghold overlooking the crossing point of the River Stour. His legions crossed the river and attacked the earthworks, which had its simple entrances blocked with masses of felled trees laid close together.

Another type of entrance is termed a 'linear hollow way'. These have a straight, parallel pair of ramparts that may turn inwards or outwards, or occasionally overlapped along the main rampart. Examples of these are illustrated above at Uley Bury, Gloucestershire where the hollow way is found leading up to the south-west corner of the hillfort.

Where a fort had two or more ramparts, it was often the custom to stagger the entrances, so that the persons entering had to turn to the left for some distance, thus exposing his unshielded sword side to defenders on the rampart above. What are termed 'complex entrances' may have

multiple overlapping outer works, staggered or interweaved multivallate ramparts, or a zig-zag entrance way that may include sling platforms with well-planned lines of fire.

The complex entrance at Caer Caradoc, Shropshire (above) shows that anyone attempting access to the fort would have to pass three banks: the inner two being in-turned, with room for defenders to rain down spears and sling shots from front, side and rear on an attacking force.

Examples of complex entrances within the Dobunnic tribal area. The top photograph (opposite page) is from Cadbury Camp, North Somerset, where the approach angles between the outer ramparts, then up though the inner rampart. To the bottom is the northern entrance to Solsbury Hill, north-east Somerset, where the approach is made through an outer horn work or ramparts which protrude from the univallate bank surrounding the

summit of the hill; the approach then parallels the inner rampart before a 90-degree left turn through the main rampart.

At Crickley Hill, Gloucestershire, a bank curves outwards from the main rampart to form a horn work reminiscent of a medieval barbican, with a gate at the outer end of it. From the top of the horn work, the defenders had complete control over everyone entering. At some excavated hillfort entrances, guard chambers have been revealed that were incorporated into the in-turned ends of the rampart. Some of them are little more than sentry box size, where others were larger, possibly where the guards could have slept and perhaps operated a watch system from. At Leckhampton Camp, Gloucestershire, two stone guard chambers, formerly thought to be rectangular in plan, were discovered on either side of the main southern entrance.

THE DOBUNNI TRIBE

The Dobunni were one of the Iron Age tribes living in the British Isles prior to the Roman invasion and are known from several references to the tribe in Roman histories and from inscriptions. The meaning of the name is unclear, but some archaeologists, such as Miles Russel, suggest that their original name may have been 'Bodunni', connected with the Celtic word 'Bouda', meaning victorious in the sense of 'victorious ones'. As an aside, the name Boudicca, the well-known famous warrior queen of the Iceni tribe from Norfolk, is also linked to the word meaning 'victory'. Author and Doctor of Philosophy Martin Counihan has proposed that the name should be interpreted as archaic Irish and means 'people at the river mouth'. This may have an element of truth, as the Dobunni tribe's geographic location was centred around modern-day Gloucestershire and the Severn estuary.

The names of the Celtic Iron Age tribes were recorded by Roman and Greek historians and geographers, including Claudius Ptolemy who lived circa AD 100 to circa AD 170 and was a mathematician, astronomer and geographer from Alexandria, Egypt. His geographical works, illustrated on the following page, are one of the main sources for the names and distribution of the British tribes.

The Dobunni tribe lived in the area of south-west Britain coinciding with the modern counties of Gloucestershire, Avon and North Somerset. At times, their territory may have extended into parts of what is now Herefordshire,

PEOPLES OF
SOUTHERN BRITAIN
BASED ON PTOLEMY'S MAP
C.150
BRIGANTES
BRIGANTES
PARISI
CORNOVII
ORDOVICES
CORIELTAUVI
ICENI
DOBUNNI
CATUVELLAUNI
TRINO-
VANTES
DEMETAE
SILURES
DOBUNNI
ATREBATES
CANTIACI
REGNI
BELGAE
DUROTRIGES
DAMNONII

Oxfordshire, North Wiltshire, Worcestershire and Warwickshire. As for the surrounding peoples, it is thought they were bordered by the Cornovii and Corieltauvi to the north; the Atrebates to the south-east and the Catuvellauni to the east; the Durotriges to the south; and the Silures and Ordovices to the west.

BRIEF ORIGINS OF EARLY BRITISH PEOPLE

What were the origins of these tribes, and especially the Dobunni people? To have an idea, it's best to go back even further than the Dobunni and the Iron Age period and appreciate the different waves of peoples who migrated west and north over millennia, eventually reaching Britain and Ireland, halting as they had essentially reached the end of the world. During what is termed the Mesolithic Age (Middle Stone Age) 11,000 years ago, following the retreat of the ice northwards, small groups of hunter gatherers, probably extended family groups, crossed the land bridge which existed between Britain and continental Europe at that time and then ranged over the largely forested countryside. The population of Britain, excluding Ireland, around 9000 BC has been estimated to have been between 1100 and 1200 people; a surprisingly small amount who hunted and foraged the countryside, constantly moving and probably very rarely encountering other groups.

Around 6000 BC, farmers who had initially been located around southern Europe and the Mediterranean, who had been gradually migrating north over generations, eventually reached Britain. The clearing of land for agriculture began and the hunter-gatherers gradually moved to the margins of the islands. This was the Neolithic Age, and its peoples were responsible for the earliest incarnations of Stonehenge and burial sites, permanent settlements and the use of polished stone implements.

Another wave of people who were living in central Europe and had previously migrated west from the Eurasian Steppe continued their migration west and finally arrived in Britain around 4400 BC. This was the Beaker culture, so-called after the bell-shaped beakers or drinking vessels which have been excavated as grave goods alongside their buried dead. The hunter-gatherers were long gone at this stage. Data suggests that over a span of several hundred years, this migration of peoples from continental Europe led to an almost complete replacement of Britain's earlier inhabitants; only 10 per cent of the population came from earlier Neolithic farmers. By the end of the Neolithic period, around 2500 BC, the population of Britain had grown to an estimated 250,000, and by the end of the Bronze Age, this number had doubled to 500,000 as the number of settlements increased along with their size, supported by improving methods of animal husbandry and agriculture.

In 2021, a major archaeogenetic study led by academics from the Universities of York, Vienna and the Harvard Medical School uncovered another migration into southern Britain during the 500-year period between 1300 and 800 BC. The newcomers were genetically most similar to ancient individuals from Gaul, in modern-day France. During 1000–875 BC, their genetic marker swiftly spread through southern Britain, making up around 50 per cent of the ancestry of subsequent Iron Age people in this area, but not in northern Britain.

In the largest such analysis published to date, scientists examined the DNA of nearly 800 ancient individuals. The combined DNA and archaeological evidence suggest that, rather than a violent invasion or a single migratory event, the genetic structure of the population changed through sustained contacts between mainland Britain and Europe over several centuries, such as the movement of traders, intermarriage and small-scale movements of family groups.

Lead archaeologist, Professor Ian Armit from the University of York comments, 'we have long suspected based on patterns of trade and shared ideologies, that the middle to late Bronze Age was a time of intense contacts between communities in Britain and Europe.' Theories held before of only a few individuals such as traders and small bands of warriors having long distance mobility in the Bronze Age have been disproved by this study, showing that considerable populations were not static but mobile, moving across the whole spectrum of society.

ESTABLISHING THE DOBUNNIC TRIBAL REGION

The map on the following page shows the distribution of coins of the Dobunni from excavated finds. The heavy concentration of coins illustrates the approximate extent of the tribal region.

The distinguished numismatist Derek Allen, combining ideas from a number of earlier sources, used distribution maps of pre-Roman coins to elaborate three points.

1: By projecting backwards in time the names of tribal groupings relating to Romano-British administration, he suggested the possibility of recognizing a pre-Roman social pattern.

2: He sought to link these political/administrative groupings with physically distinctive and discretely distributed sets of pre-Roman coins.

3: He then mapped these projected distributions as cultural territories.

From this work, Derek Allen marked the territory using the distribution of Dobunnic coinage, placing the nucleus of the tribal region

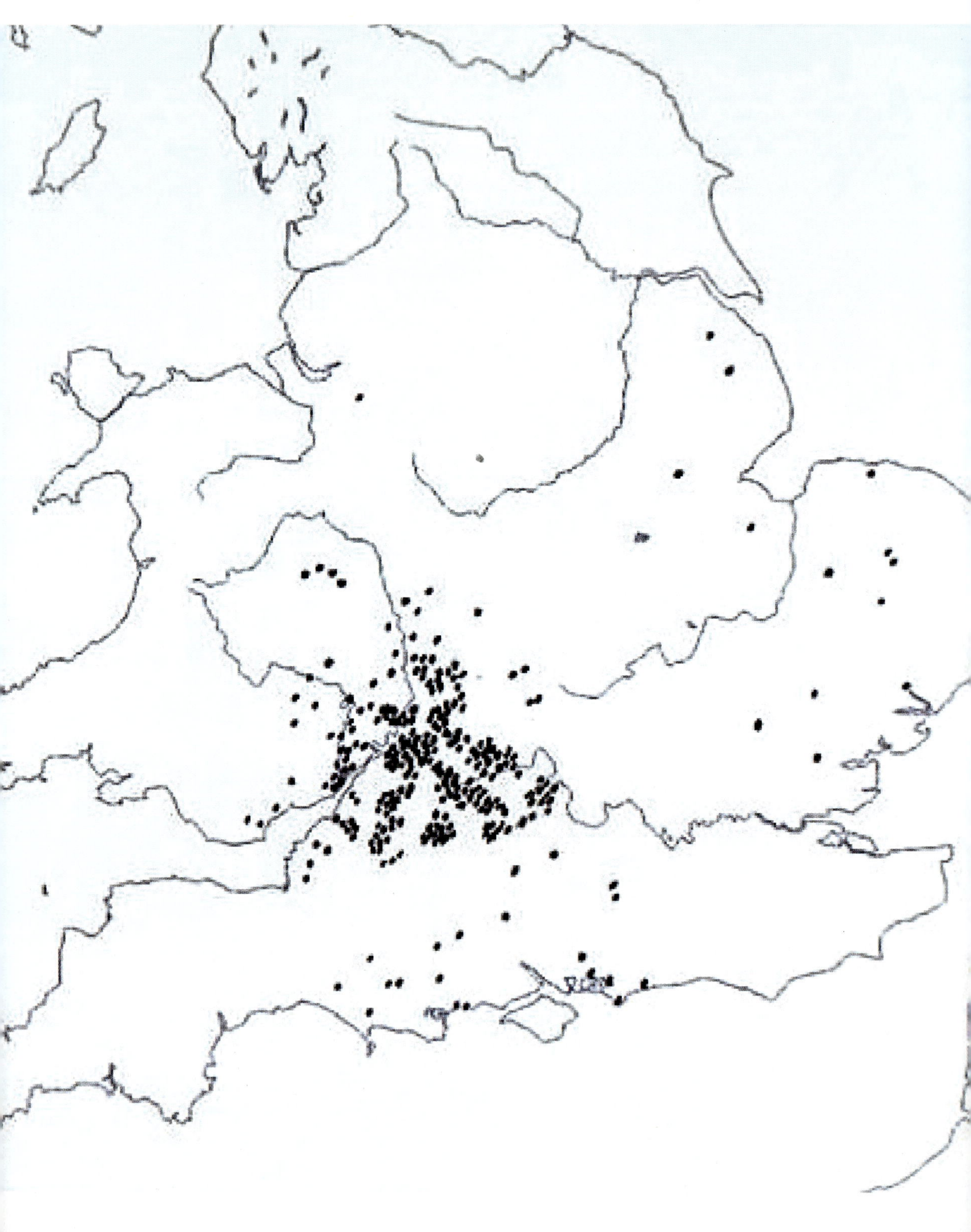

in Gloucestershire. The capital of the territory has been established at Bagendon, some 5km north-west of modern-day Cirencester, now just an idyllic Cotswold village nestled in rolling hills; but back 2500 years ago, it had an extensive population and was a major industrial and trading centre. The areas of Dobunnic territory which lay close to the expanding influence of the Trinovantes and Catuvellauni, particularly the east Cotswolds where Bagendon is located, developed earthworks similar to the Oppida of the south-east of Britain. Oppida literally means 'walled town' and is defined as a 'defended town with an economy largely dependent on semi-industrialized manufacturing and trade'. In the south-east of Britain during the first century BC, hilltop fortifications went out of general use, and there appears to be a shift of the population to valley side sites, often to positions which controlled river crossings and trade. They were often tribal capitals, as was the case with Bagendon, Gloucestershire which was a site located on a promontory of some 81ha and was partly enclosed by linear ditches. Following the Roman invasion and subsequent occupation, the Oppida at Bagendon became redundant as the Romans developed Corinium Dobunnorum, present-day Cirencester, which became their capital of the Cotswolds.

In the photograph below, we are looking north over the Bagendon oppidum. The highlighted lines are where the banks and ditches are still visible or were situated and have been destroyed over time by agriculture and ploughing.

The exact territorial boundaries for each of the tribes is unknown, but using the research of archaeologists and using evidence of pre-Roman coin distribution, topography and the location of hillforts, boundaries can be formulated to some degree. Using the information mentioned previously I have developed a theory concerning the geographic extent of the Dobunnic region. I must stress that this is just a theory I am putting forwards, I may be well off-target, but I believe it is a reasonable assumption using the available sources and my own research.

The western boundary follows the natural border provided by the River Wye flowing south from Herefordshire into the Severn Estuary at Chepstow. Northwards, the tribal territory extends up to the River Teme, which flows east to west from the Welsh hills through the rolling hills of Herefordshire and Worcestershire before it joins the Severn just north of the Malvern Hills at Worcester. In the south, the border runs east from the Bristol Channel along the line of the Mendip Hills and the hills of North Somerset, continuing along the chalk uplands of the northern edge of the Vale of Pewsey. The border proceeds north-east along the chalk uplands of north Wiltshire which then continue east through the rolling hills of south Oxfordshire. The easternmost extent of the territory uses the natural border of the River Thames, and the River Cherwell provides the north-eastern boundary as it flows north to south before joining the Thames at Oxford.

These borders are not fixed and definite, and there may have been large areas which were in effect no man's land between settlements and different tribal regions. This may have been due to a variety of reasons: thick forest, swamps and marshy ground, areas which were not agriculturally viable and so not worth tension and conflict over. Boundaries were not in straight lines as we have in modern times; the closest that would resemble this would be the tribal boundary following a river. Many communities were small and relatively isolated from the nearest neighbours, so the map would resemble jigsaw pieces, with the area around each community being farmed and worked with large areas around them empty due to the various reasons previously discussed. The particular size of a settlement combined with its topographical and geographic position seems to have dictated the size of the area it not necessarily controlled, but had an influence on agriculture and land use. Hence, a small, enclosed farmstead would, at one end of the scale, be the centre of a handful of square kilometres, enough land to support an extended family; while the developed hillforts in the first millennium, which appear to be centres of tribal territories or regional capitals, possibly influenced an area of 80-100 sq. km (30-40 square miles).

SOCIETY AND RELIGION

There are two hypotheses with regard to the aristocratic class of Iron Age Britain as to where they lived with their families and retainers. The question is whether they permanently occupied hillforts and directed control from these centres. This would have been the equivalent of a medieval baronial castle where the lord resided, tithes were stored and servants lived and worked. The alternate view is that the ruling class used the hillfort as a meeting place where tribal business was carried out, but then the leaders would retire to a large farmstead where their families resided. The answer to this question may depend on a number of factors; the main one being that the Dobunnic period spanned hundreds of years through times of peace and prosperity to those of war and conflict, whether local or when the problem became regional following the Roman invasion of AD 43. When times were good and peace reigned, the climate was kind, harvests flourished and the population increased, possibly the aristocratic class did retire to their homesteads dotted around their

regional capitals. However, when times were harder, harvests failed and tensions with neighbours increased, the population, including the aristocrats, may then have looked at hunkering down within the walls of their local hillforts.

Apart from the 'aristocratic' warrior class of the chieftains and their liege men, the vast majority of the population would have been made up predominantly of farmers working the land, creating produce for the immediate community, with any surplus being traded or stored for winter and potential harder times. Those of the population not working the land would be made up of traders, metal and leather workers, and other craftsmen of Iron Age society.

Stephen Yeates, author of The Tribe of Witches: The Religion of the Dobunni and Hwicce, asserts that a study of the religious practices of the Dobunni has shown that there was a focus on the worship of the natural world. Sacred locations would have been found at springs, bogs and rivers, as well as other natural features, such as very old trees or groves of trees. Iron Age people believed the gods lived in these places and had to be served and honoured by ritual practices. In Gloucestershire, it is possible to identify deities associated with the landscape; for example, the mother goddess Cuda, venerated as the spirit of place, to whom worshippers gave thanks for the abundance of the Cotswold Valleys with its rivers and springs. Sculptures still exist of Cuda in the form of a seated mother with apples in her lap. She personifies the generous and abundant spirit of the land. Shrines were established on rivers, particularly at their sources, such as the Thames in Gloucestershire. A major shrine associated with metal working was established at Lydney Park, Gloucestershire. Mineral sources were revered, and offerings were made at the end of worked-out mines; this was in the belief that, like a tree, the mineral would regrow.

As we have established, the Dobunnic tribal territory through the first millennium BC was quite extensive. However, in the last two decades before the Roman invasion 20-43 AD, the territory seems to have split into two ruling households. Comux, followed by Bodvoc, controlled the northern region of Herefordshire, Gloucestershire, Worcestershire and Oxfordshire, while Corio remained dominant in northern Somerset. The division can be traced in the native pottery and its distribution in the first century BC. North of the Bristol Avon, the principal types included jars and saucepan shapes decorated with a zone of either linear tooling or stamping below the rim. These have been shown to have been manufactured in the Malvern area and exported widely. The north Somerset region, on the other hand, developed a totally different style of ceramics influenced partly by the new technological developments in the Durotrigian region to the south. This style is called 'Glastonbury ware' and is characterized by necked bowls, saucepan pots and simple beaded, rimmed jars.

This factional political situation among the Dobunni at the time of the Roman invasion can also be reflected in their coinage. The northern region was headed by Bodvoc, whose coins were modelled on Roman types, suggesting a potential pro-Roman attitude. South of the River Avon in north Somerset, the more traditional coinage of Corio was dominant. This division between the two types of coinage could be interpreted as representing pro-Roman and anti-Roman factions. It has been suggested that by 43 AD, the northern region, centred on Gloucestershire, was coming under the domination of the Catuvellauni tribe and was therefore more willing to throw in its lot with Rome. Corio, in north Somerset, may well have fended off south-eastern aggression and have been less inclined to side with the invaders. In time, both territories came under the heel of Roman occupation and were garrisoned as part of the military frontier zone based on the line of the Fosse Way running parallel to the River Severn-Trent axis.

An interesting aspect of the political separation of the Dobunni is the situation along the new frontier that existed between the two factions along the River Avon, and especially as the river flows through the Avon Gorge

in modern-day Bristol. Where Bristol Suspension Bridge now stands, there are three hillforts located on either side of the gorge. These forts are not defending the bridge, but an ancient ford across the Avon below, where the bridge now stands. In Iron Age times at low tide, a ridge of rock was uncovered across the river, which provided the crossing, and the forts at Clifton Camp on the north of the gorge and Burgh Walls and Stokeleigh on the southern side were ideally located to administer and defend the crossing if necessary. The site of modern-day Bristol to the east of the gorge around the Avon would have been a marshy low-lying area, which made this crossing an important trade route. However, after the tribe split, this area may have become a potential flash point, with rival factions viewing each other across the gorge. The low tide ridge of rock creating the ford was destroyed in the nineteenth century to allow larger vessels into the Port of Bristol as trade flourished and the port expanded.

The ford across the Avon was located approximately below where the suspension bridge spans today. Clifton Camp, in the above photograph, is an inland promontory fort located on the north cliff edge of the Avon Gorge. The ring of trees in the image below follows the line of banks and ditches which are still visible as shown in photo four.

Stokeleigh Camp, located on the southern edge of the Avon Gorge in Leigh Woods, is another promontory fort with the steep-sided Nightingale Valley to the east and an indented combe of the Avon Gorge providing natural defence on two sides. The fort is protected on its landward side by a double arc of defensive ramparts and ditches. Unfortunately, the third hillfort, named Burgh Walls, another promontory fort located at the southern end of the suspension bridge, has been largely destroyed by development; villas were built on the site from 1868 onwards.

Parking in Leigh Woods to visit Stokeleigh Camp is found in North Road (what3words: glad.arrow.much). Or to take in both Clifton and Stokeleigh Camps, park as I did on Ladies Mile, Clifton Downs (what3words: faced. helps.drill), which is free, and walk along the edge of the Avon Gorge, then cross the suspension bridge. The walk is 8.8km in length; difficulty three. Café at the Clifton Observatory has spectacular views from both sides of the Avon Gorge and from the bridge.

HILLFORTS OF GLOUCESTERSHIRE

For this project, I am using the historic boundaries of Gloucestershire, which encompass the modern unitary authority of South Gloucestershire and extend down into the city of Bristol to the River Avon. Gloucestershire and the Cotswold hills that run north to south along the edge of the Severn Vale were the centre of the Dobunnic tribal region. The natural border running along the River Wye to the west is the only frontier with a neighbouring tribe: the Silurians in what is now South Wales. However, the county is covered with hillforts and Iron Age settlements dating back to the times of the initial establishment of boundaries.

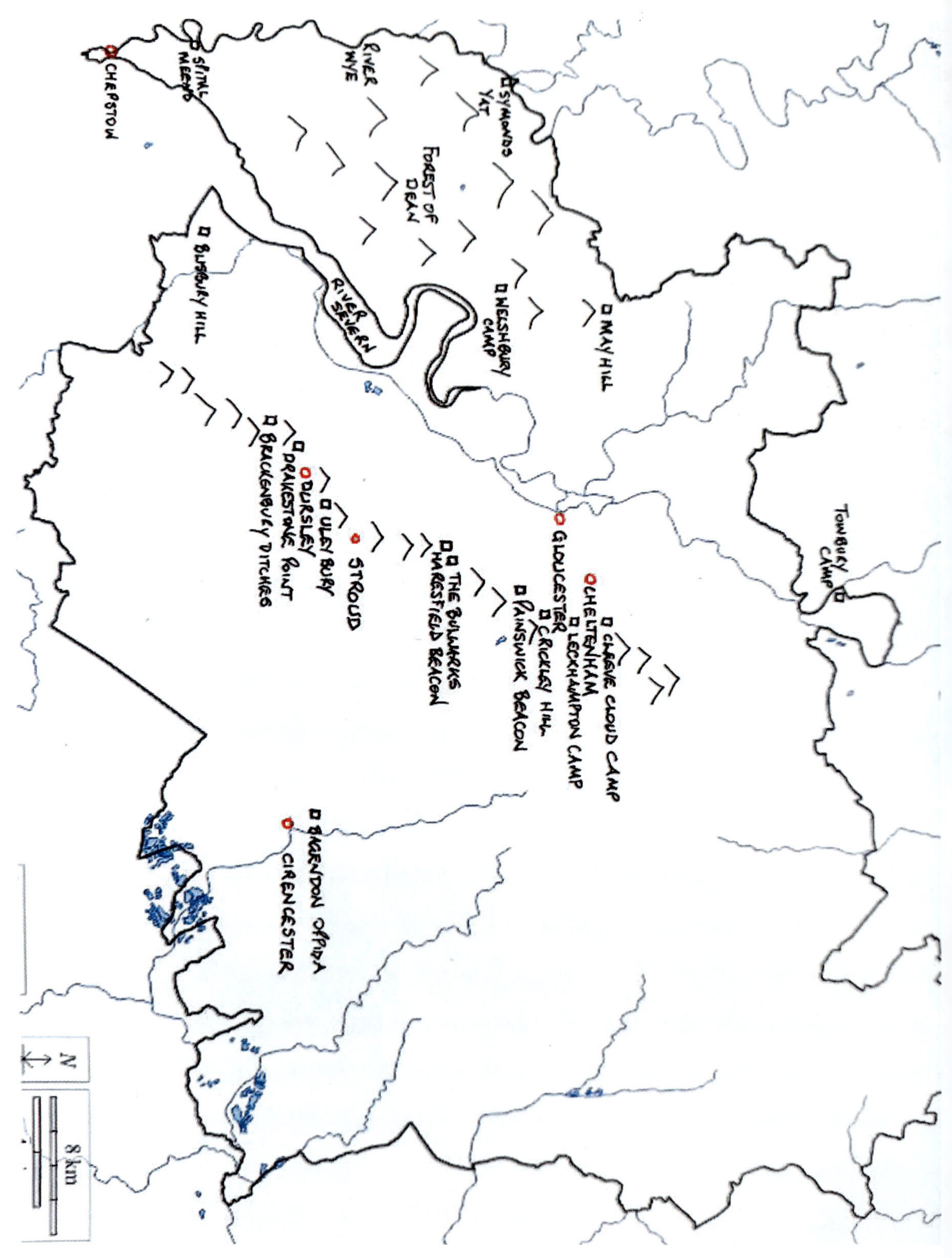

Map of the hillforts in South Gloucestershire and the Bristol area.

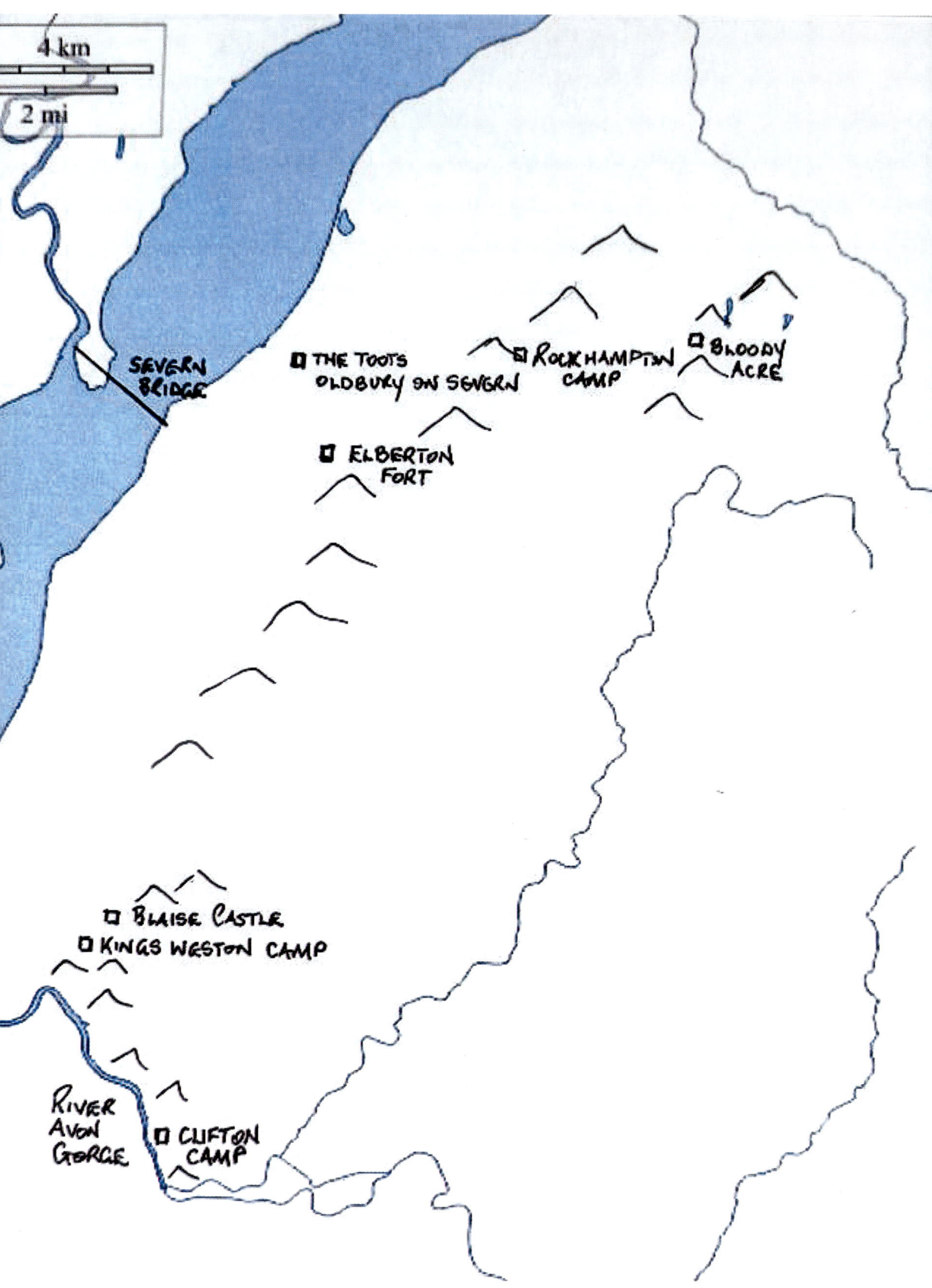

4 km
2 mi
SEVERN BRIDGE
THE TOOTS
OLDBURY ON SEVERN
ROCKHAMPTON CAMP
BLOODY ACRE
ELBERTON FORT
BLAISE CASTLE
KINGS WESTON CAMP
RIVER AVON GORGE
CLIFTON CAMP

ULEY BURY

The Bury stands at 230m above sea level and commands spectacular views of the Severn Vale, across to the Forest of Dean, and into South Wales, and lies within the Cotswold 'Area of Outstanding Natural Beauty' (AONB).

The fort itself is a large sub-rectangular partial contour hillfort with very steep slopes on all sides, apart from a narrow neck of land (col) to the north, connecting the fort to the Cotswold scarp which runs north to south bisecting Gloucestershire. The site measures 600m by 200m and encloses an area of 16ha, with a generally flat interior. The earthworks are bivallate on all sides with a possible third rampart on the south-west slope and were

Looking at the south-west side of the Bury, looking north up the Cotswold escarpment.

created by terracing a double line of ramparts, more than 1.5km in length into the hillsides. There are entrances at the north, east and south corners with hollow ways to the south and east.

Finds from excavations at the east entrance in 1976 prior to pipeline laying uncovered Iron Age pottery, a bronze ring-headed pin, two shale armulets and glass beads. During the laying of the pipe, a Roman or Sub-Roman crouched burial between two layers of limestone slabs, a rubbish pit and two Iron Age currency bars were unearthed. Other finds include an uninscribed gold stater of the Dobunni found in 1885; this was a premium coin type of Celtic culture, first appearing in Britain around 150 BC, made of a mix of metals, predominantly gold with silver and copper (in Gloucester Museum). A Roman quern stone, used since ancient times to grind grain and carried by Roman legionaries on campaign, was found (now in Stroud Museum), as was a low-relief bronze mask (in Corinium Museum).

The Bury from the west.

Looking south, showing the Bury in the distance and its commanding position with steep slopes on all sides.

A small car park is located at the north entrance, just off B4066, at the top of Crawley Hill, running north out of Uley village (what3words: assure. questions.because). A circular walk of 1.5 km, relatively flat; difficulty one.

An alternative is to park in the village of Uley, street parking near the church (what3words: shifters.notebook.relieves). A footpath leads up the hill from behind the church. This is a more challenging walk of 3.3km, difficulty four, but can be rewarded with a drink afterwards in the Crown Inn opposite the church. The Cotswold Way footpath skirts the west side of the fort. Landranger map 162. Map ref. NGR 785989.

KIMSBURY CAMP, PAINSWICK BEACON, CASTLE GODWIN

Painswick Beacon, also known as Kimsbury Camp and Castle Godwin, is a triangular-shaped, bivallate, partial contour fort sited on a south-west-facing spur of the Cotswold escarpment. It has steep surrounding slopes, more moderate to the north-east, and encloses 1.9ha and stands at an altitude of 283m. The earthworks comprise two closely set banks and two ditches with a visible counterscarp on the west, south and east sides. The interior has been extensively

quarried and sections are now part of the golf course, however, much remains of the ramparts. There are four gaps which could be entrances; however, the possible original main in-turned entrance is found towards the south-east corner. This is where the main visible footpath bisects the earthworks in the previous page photo.

The site has been dated to the first century BC and is a scheduled monument. Pottery, coins and other archaeological finds, including a rusty sword and spear heads, have been excavated dating from the Iron Age through to the third century AD in the Roman era. The Cotswold Way runs adjacent to the fort and can be followed to Crickley Hill to the north and Haresfield Beacon to the south.

Painswick Beacon is signposted from both A46 and B4073 heading north out of Painswick. There is a large parking area with many paths accessing the much-quarried hill spur that rolls green and dramatic up to

Viewed from the north (*previous page*) and north-east (*above*), showing the less-steep slopes.

the hillfort (what3words: stocks.aura.saves). A trig point is found on the highest point of the rampart standing at 283m. It is a short walk of 1km, difficulty two/three, including a circuit of the earthworks. Try to avoid any golf balls, but enjoy the spectacular views. Landranger map 162. Map ref. NGR 869121.

CRICKLEY HILL

Overlooking the Severn Vale, the city of Gloucester and the Malvern Hills to the north, Crickley Hill is a promontory hillfort situated on a west-facing spur of the Cotswold escarpment. There is evidence of numerous periods of occupation from the neolithic of 3700 BC to post-Roman of the fifth century AD and is considered a site of international historical importance.

Roughly triangular in shape with very steep surrounding slopes to the north, west and south, with a more moderate slope along the ridge to the east. A single bank and ditch cut off the promontory in a curving line running north to south.

In neolithic times, there is evidence that the site was used for worship, particularly in the area of the 'long mound', which had a shrine, a stone

circle and processional way used for rituals and religious purposes from 3700-500 BC. About 5500 years ago, (occupation of) the settlement ended in violence, when 400 flint-tipped arrow heads were discovered with evidence of houses and a gateway burnt, making Crickley Hill the site of one of the first known battlefields in the country.

The settlement was replaced in the early Iron Age, possibly seventh century BC, with what is still visible today, a rubble-cored, timber-laced rampart enclosing an area of some 3.9ha. A rock-cut (the limestone is inches below the surface), flat-bottomed ditch would have run parallel to the rampart. This hillfort again was burnt and slighted from an attacking force and abandoned. The next phase of occupation refortified 75m of the ramparts north and south of the entrance and reconstructed the entrance with large out-turned horn work with solid stone bastions at the gate. However, the site was again destroyed by fire and abandoned. It was later

reoccupied in the late Iron Age within the original ramparts. Excavated finds include neolithic sherds and local pottery of the early and late Iron Age.

The hillfort is located within Crickley Hill Country Park, which enjoys shared ownership with the National Trust and Gloucestershire Wildlife Trust. The site has a large car park, café and circular walks offering spectacular views (what3words: spark.barrel.glider). A circular walk of the hillfort and Country Park is approximately 3.5km; difficulty two. Landranger map 163. Map ref. NGR 928161.

HARESFIELD HILL CAMP, RING HILL & THE BULWARKS

Haresfield Hill Camp is a partial contour/promontory hillfort located at the end of a west-facing spur of the Cotswold escarpment on Haresfield Beacon. The camp is surrounded by very steep slopes to south-east, south and north-west, and a moderate slope to the east on the ridge of the spur, with considerable ramparts of some 5m in height following the crest of the natural ridge above a gully

Looking south-west over the promontory with the ramparts in the tree line in the foreground.

A view looking towards the substantive ramparts in the treeline from inside the fort.

THE BULWARKS

The Bulwarks consists of a single curving bank with an outer ditch crossing the neck of the spur 576m east of Haresfield Hill Camp. To the north and south, the surrounding slopes are very steep. The bank is 14m wide and 2m high of glacis construction with the outer ditch 12m wide and some 2m deep. Very little is known about these earthworks, but perhaps they were an outer defence for Haresfield Hill Camp and or a protected area for cattle and livestock outside of the main settlement. The Bulwarks are on private land with no footpaths or public access; however, the bank and ditch can be seen from the road. The Cotswold Way passes to the north but contours along the escarpment further down the slope in the surrounding woods.

Park at the National Trust car park (what3words: advantage.drain.blinks) and walk along the lane towards the Beacon, or drive further down to the limited parking near the fort (what3words: assembles.waxes.weekends). The walk from the NT car park with a circular walk of the fort is 3.5km; difficulty two. Landranger 162 Map Ref. NGR 823090.

The photo above shows the Bulwarks in the tree line along the foreground with Haresfield Hill Camp extending out onto the promontory. The photo below shows the bank in the tree line, standing 2m in height.

LECKHAMPTON CAMP

Sitting atop the prominent north-west-facing ridge at the edge of the limestone plateau and escarpment overlooking the Severn Vale and the Regency town of Cheltenham is the univallate, inland promontory fort of Leckhampton Camp. The camp stands at an elevation of 285m and is protected naturally by vertical cliffs and very steep slopes to the north and west, with a curving single rampart beginning from the cliffs to the north, initially running south, then curving to the west. The outer ditch is visible at the northern end of the bank, but elsewhere in-filled with debris, so no longer apparent.

A study of the rampart, ditch and entrances was carried out in 1969-1971 by Sara Champion. During these excavations, the bank was found to be 6m wide and 1.8m in height, with the ditch, having to be rock-cut, being 2.7m deep. There was evidence of charcoal and burnt wood within the rampart, so much so that the heat had reddened the limestone. This was similar to the evidence found in the ramparts and entrances at Crickley Hill a few miles to the south. Were these attacks on both settlements linked to some sort of regional conflict? It raises questions, but we will never know the detail of what really happened.

At the north-east apex is a complex in-turned entrance with two stone guard chambers flanking the passage. A bowl barrow within a square enclosure is located outside the ramparts by this entrance, which is not always obvious to the walker but can be appreciated more when viewed from the top of the rampart. The circular mound is 10m in diameter and 0.6m in height with a hollowed centre, and is surrounded by a square enclosure defined by a bank standing 0.6m in height. It has been dated to the late Neolithic between 2400-1500 BC. Excavations have produced two human skeletons of possible Iron Age date, but no direct link could be found between the barrow and the hillfort.

Chance finds of pottery have indicated multiple phases of occupancy, including the Iron Age, Romano-British, Anglo-Saxon and medieval periods.

This view is from the west looking at the limestone cliffs of the Cotswold escarpment, which provide natural defence.

The aerial view is looking at the fort from the east and shows the curving single rampart. In the foreground outside of the rampart, the square enclosure can be seen with the bowl barrow within it.

Turn right off the Ullenwood to Leckhampton Road into Hartley Lane and the car park is in a disused quarry on the left (what3words: cuddled. acrobat.routine). There is a circular 2km walk with an initial climb out of the quarry; difficulty two. Landranger map 163. Map ref. NGR 947183

CLEEVE CLOUD CAMP, CLEEVE HILL

Overlooking the Regency town of Cheltenham, located on the plateau edge of Cleeve Hill, Cleeve Cloud Camp is a bivallate promontory hillfort. The ramparts are formed of two series of banks and ditches enclosing an area of 1.2ha of a slight promontory of gently sloping ground, extending for some 100m to the scarp edge. There are very steep slopes offering natural defence to the west and south, as seen in the photograph below. The fort stands at an elevation of 300m. Cleeve Hill, at 330m, is the highest point in Gloucestershire and of the Cotswold Hill range.

The banks and ditches have been disturbed by quarrying, and to the north the outer defences have been cut through to create a green for the golf course which occupies Cleeve Hill. Apart from the modern-day damage, the banks and ditches are still impressive, with the banks standing some 2.5-3m above the ditches. Unfortunately, no entrance survives. The fort has been dated to late Bronze Age to early Iron Age, 800-600 BC. Evidence of human activity on Cleeve Common has been traced back some 6000 years with flint scatters, at least one neolithic long barrow and a cross dyke all visible north of the hillfort.

From the south, the car park is accessed from Cheltenham via Ham Hill and Aggs Hill, which are steep single-track lanes. The car park is located near to the summit trig point (what3words: homecare.summaries.mirroring) and is a walk of 2km; difficulty two. Alternatively, from the north travelling from Cheltenham, turn right off the B4632 signposted Cleeve Hill Golf Club; public parking is located further on past the golf club car park in a disused quarry (what3words: hero.prominent.turkeys). This walk is 3km in length, difficulty three, with some climbing, but passes by the cross dyke and the Ring: an ancient settlement, possibly a fortified homestead. The Cotswold Way footpath bisects Cleeve Common, then runs along the scarp edge. Landranger map 163. Map ref. NGR 984255.

BRACKENBURY DITCHES

The name 'Brackenbury Ditches' appears first only on Ordnance Survey maps circa 1880, but around the year 1630 it was known as 'Becketsbury', a term not now used. A roughly triangular, Iron Age inland promontory fort, Brackenbury Ditches is located on the south-west end of a steep sided spur above the village of North Nibley. Bivallate glacis banks and ditches curve from the north-west to the south-east, with the ends resting on the scarp edge enclose an area of 3.2ha with steep slopes to the south, west and north-west. The inner defensive rampart is 15m wide with a height of 3m. There has been ongoing work to clear woodland and scrub from the earthworks, which can now be viewed quite clearly.

A single bank, ditch and counterscarp run along the edge of the promontory scarp face, as seen in the photograph above with the bank to the right. An entrance is located halfway along the southern side of the single bank. There have been chance finds of Bronze Age metalwork and a tanged (sharp extension of metal blade) dagger or spearhead was found in 1904.

The (nearby Tyndale) monument was built in honour of William Tyndale, an early translator of the New Testament into English who was born nearby at Melksham Court, Stinchcombe. He was arrested in 1535, charged with heresy and executed in 1536 by strangulation, followed by his body being burnt at the stake. The tower was constructed in 1866 and stands 111 feet (34m) tall and is open to the public.

Parking is adjacent to the village cemetery in North Nibley (what3words: incorrect.scarecrow.thrilled). The walk is initially steep, climbing up the escarpment to the plateau where Tyndale Monument is located. Following the Cotswold Way to the south through woodland, you will arrive at the hillfort and see the cleared earthworks. The walk is 3km in length, difficulty three/four, with the Black Horse pub in North Nibley

for refreshments at the end of the walk. Landranger map 162. Map ref. NGR 747948.

A view looking north from the fort towards Tyndale Monument, with the village of North Nibley below.

SYMONDS YAT HILLFORT

Located on the north-west-facing headland of Symonds Yat Rock in the Forest of Dean, high above a large loop of the River Wye, is the inland promontory Iron Age hillfort of Symonds Yat. Triangular in shape, the hillfort stands 122m above the river, with precipitous cliffs to the west, north and east providing natural defence. The promontory is cut off in the south by a series of five banks and four ditches enclosing an area of 4.4ha.

The view below is looking south, showing the triangular shape of the hillfort, with the steep slopes/cliffs on three sides with the River Wye looping below again providing a natural barrier.

This view above, taken above the hillfort, looks north. The tree line indicates the fort's triangular shape, with the large loop of the River Wye extending into the background.

The most southerly and outermost line of defence and the next two northwards consist of banks fronted with V-shaped ditches. The ditches are 4.5m wide with the banks rising up to 2m in height. The two earthworks providing the inner defence are a pair of banks with a ditch between them. These works have been popularly attributed to King Offa, who reigned from 784-796 AD. His dyke, a defensive structure consisting of a substantial bank and ditch running from the Severn Estuary to Liverpool

Bay, separated the Welsh kingdom of Powys from the Anglian kingdom of Mercia. However, there are no sections of the dyke associated with the hillfort, and the nature of the defences and pottery finds from the site firmly date it to the Iron Age.

There have been late Iron Age pottery finds and fragments of tap-slag, suggesting bloomery smelting on the site. This was the earliest form of smelter producing iron in a solid state; this is because the bloomery process was conducted at a temperature lower than the melting point of iron ore. Carbon monoxide from the incomplete combustion of charcoal slowly diffused through the hot iron oxide ore, converting it to iron metal and carbon dioxide.

The photographs on this page show Symonds Yat Rock from the east with the viewing point visible just off centre, and then viewed from the west.

This area is a popular and spectacular tourist attraction. There is a large car park (what3words: dating.clasping.final), log cabin café and viewing point on the rock to take in the glorious views of the River Wye below. The viewing point is a popular spot for ornithologists observing and photographing nesting pairs of peregrine falcons and other birds of prey. The walk from the car park to the café and viewing point cuts through the earthworks so they can be easily seen and is level; a difficulty one. Walks can be extended down the hillside, with the Saracens Head Hotel providing refreshments riverside, with a steep climb back to the car park. Landranger map 162. Map ref. NGR 563157.

DRAKESTONE CAMP

Drakestone Camp is an inland promontory fort located on the south-west-facing spur of Drakestone Point, overlooking the Severn Vale below and Stinchcombe Hill and golf course to the north-east. Banks and ditches cut off the promontory enclosing a small area of 0.04ha. The area is too small for a camp/ settlement. Suggested theories include it being used as a look out and or a signalling post, as it has spectacular 360-degree views, but then why did it have such heavy-duty defences? We will never know for certain.

These photos are looking west over Drakestone Camp to the River Severn in the distance. A last photograph is taken from the ditch looking at the not-inconsiderable inner bank.

This hillfort is definitely worth a visit for the views alone. Car parking is 1km away from the fort on the top of Stinchcombe Hill. Drive past the golf to the car park (what3words: rocket.postings.someone). Difficulty one. Landranger map 162. Map Ref. NGR 736980.

MAY HILL

Located on the prominent summit of May Hill in the Forest of Dean, standing at an elevation of 296m, this hillfort is distinguishable for miles around by a clump of trees on the summit. It is a possible contour hillfort with a bank and ditch measuring 145m in diameter; within this area is a mound that is said to be a round barrow. The earthworks do not look substantial enough for necessarily defensive means, but may have been an enclosure for religious rituals, feasting and festivals; its importance and significance are highlighted by being located on such a prominent summit. May Hill is visible for miles around in all directions, from the Herefordshire Hills to the north, down the Severn Vale to the south and across to the Cotswold Hills to the east.

There are parking spaces adjacent to Glasshouse village green (what3words: meanings.photocopy.branch) with Glasshouse public house just along the road for refreshments post-walk. Follow the Wysis Way footpath from Glasshouse up through the woods. It's a 4.5km round walk, difficulty 3, but worth the effort for the views.

OLD SODBURY CAMP

Old Sodbury Camp is a large multivallate hillfort located on the summit of a small ridge on the edge of the Cotswold escarpment, with commanding views over the Severn Vale and over to the Welsh Mountains. To the west the escarpment drops below the rampart with steep slopes; in all other directions, the ground is relatively flat. The hillfort is roughly rectangular, measuring 277m by 190m, enclosing an area of 9.48ha. There are widely spaced double ramparts and ditches on all but the west side, where there is a single bank and berm above the escarpment. The outer rampart is 17m wide and 3m high, with the outer ditch 13m wide and 3m deep. There is a causewayed entrance on the eastern side.

Eight Roman coins were excavated in the interior ranging from Emperor Gallienus 253-268 AD to Constantius II 337-361 AD. The Romans used the earthworks as a stronghold with its favourable position protecting their western frontier. King Edward IV and his army camped within the earthworks prior to the Yorkist victory over Margaret of Anjou at the Battle of Tewkesbury in 1471.

For a circular walk incorporating both Old Sodbury and Horton Camp (see next profile), park at Horton Camp (what3words: litters.envisage.skips). Follow signs for the Cotswold Way, which drops down into the village of Horton and Little Sodbury, then climbs up to Old Sodbury fort. Return via the top path and the lane. The walk is 6km, difficulty three. Landranger map 172. Map ref. NGR 760825.

HORTON CAMP, THE CASTLES

Horton Camp, also known as 'The Castles', is a univallate inland promontory fort situated on a south-west-facing spur of the Cotswold escarpment. There are steep slopes to the south and west, though relatively flat to north and east, with a curving rampart cutting off the promontory. It is roughly D-shaped, measuring 203m by 158m, enclosing an area of 2.78ha. The rampart is 12m wide and 3m in height, with a ditch which is now a buried feature some 7m wide. There are three entrances that have been identified: the one on the north-east almost halfway round the rampart may have been an

original one, but has since been levelled for farming purposes. To the south-west and north are hollow way entrances.

Parking is in a layby next to the adjacent field (what3words: litters. envisage.skips) with a signpost showing the path. It is a short walk of less than 1km; difficulty one. Landranger map 172. Map ref. NGR 764843.

DYRHAM CAMP, HINTON HILLFORT

Situated on the summit of Hinton Hill on the tip of a south-west-facing spur of the Cotswold escarpment is the univallate partial contour fort of Dyrham Camp. It is roughly triangular in shape, with steep slopes to the south-east, south and west, with moderate slopes to the north and east. The dimensions of the hillfort are 310m long and 229m wide, enclosing an area of 4.8ha. The fort is bisected with a road leading up from the village of Hinton in the valley below to the A46 in the east. The single rampart is most visible to the east being 2.4m in height and 10m wide, with an outer ditch measuring 6m wide and 1.5m deep, cutting off the promontory from the gentle slopes leading down from the Cotswold plateau. The southern edge of the

Looking west over Dyrham Camp, with the east-facing rampart and ditch being the best preserved.

fort above the escarpment still retains the rampart but the northern earthworks are largely ploughed out and wooded with the ditch a buried feature.

Dyrham Camp is the possible site for a battle in 577 AD between the ever-expanding Saxon kingdoms and the resident Britons. It was a cataclysmic defeat for the Britons with the loss of three kings slain in battle and the Saxons of the kingdom of Wessex reaching the River Severn, thereby cutting the British kingdoms to the north and south in two. Culturally and linguistically, the kingdom of Dumnonia was severed from the British tribes in Wales and each became increasingly isolated as a result of this battle.

There is no available parking near the hillfort; however, park at Dyrham Park, which is owned by the National Trust. A visit can take in the stately home and café, and then walk up through the deer park to Dyrham Camp. The walk is 3.5km; difficulty three. Landranger map 172. Map ref. NGR 741767.

BLAISE CASTLE AND KINGS WESTON CAMP

Blaise Castle a multivallate, partial contour fort that occupies a commanding position on the north-west side of the limestone ravine of the heavily wooded Hazel Brook. There are steep surrounding slopes, especially to the south-east where there are limestone cliffs leading down to the brook. To the north and west are three substantial concentric banks and ditches which rise some 25m from the base of the first earthwork to the summit. On the southern side,

the precipitous slopes may have been deemed sufficient as there are no signs of earthworks. The fort encloses an area of 2.4ha.

The area is now a public park and golf course. Blaise Castle folly which is found in the interior of the earthworks was built by Thomas Farr (who had investments in the slave trade) in the eighteenth century to have an improved view of his trading ships as they sailed up the River Avon to Bristol.

Excavated finds include neolithic flint fragments and stone axe heads from 3000 BC to Roman coins from the later emperors Vespasian, Constantius and others, illustrating the extensive timeline of human occupation of the site. Amongst Iron Age finds include a saddle quern, twenty-four sling stones and a bone weaving comb, all held in Bristol Museum.

Located 300m to the south-west of Blaise Castle dropping down into a wooded saddle, then climbing up onto the north-eastern end of a ridge of Kings Weston Hill, is Kings Weston Camp, shown in the photograph below.

The camp is a univallate, partial contour fort with steep slopes off the ridge to the north and east with a moderate slope running along the ridge to the south-west. The rampart and ditch facing west across the ridge is the most vulnerable side, in the open, while the other ramparts run along the top of the slope in the tree line.

The area enclosed within the earthworks measures 0.4ha. Perhaps this was a defended enclosure taking advantage of the local topography just outside the main hillfort of Blaise Castle.

A large paying car park (what3words: expect.harsh.diner) is located off Kings Weston Road for Blaise Castle Public Park and café from which you look south towards the wooded slopes of the hillfort. A round walk of both sites is 2km; difficulty two/three. Landranger map 172. Map ref. NGR 558783.

OTHER HILLFORTS IN GLOUCESTERSHIRE

The above list of the most prominent and potentially the best to visit hillfort sites is not exhaustive for the area. There are many others which are on private land with no public access, or they may be denuded, partly destroyed through quarrying, ploughing out or, heaven forbid, development, and are not worth the effort to seek out. However, ever the keen historian enjoys a challenge, and be it on private land with the use of a drone the hillfort in question can be viewed in all its glory while physically not trespassing. A case in point is Bloody Acre, a multivallate contour hillfort situated in the private grounds of the Tortworth Estate in South Gloucestershire as seen below.

Many of these smaller, less well-known sites are worth a look if you enjoy a challenge while out on a walk and know what you are looking for. For the average member of the public out for a stroll, banks, ditches and entrances would be ignored as the lay of the land. However, if you are aware of a site and set out to explore the ground in question, the landscape gradually begins to make sense, and with a little imagination can be seen as it may have looked some 2500 years ago, clear of trees with the earthworks and ditches in prime condition. An example of this can be found at High Brotheridge, Cranham and Cranham Corner earthworks. Both of these are densely wooded sites, but when the ground is walked, the landscape you are seeking becomes clear. This is the same for the wooded sites at Elberton near Thornbury and Welshbury in the Forest of Dean.

The remnants of banks and ditches at Welshbury Camp, Gloucestershire, can be seen at here. Steep sides provide natural defences to north and east of the camp, with triple ramparts and ditches on the south-west and north-west quadrants. The area is now heavily wooded, but the earthworks are still in good condition to view. The walk is 3.8km; difficulty two; with parking off road, at the start of forest track located between the villages of Flaxley and Mitcheldean (what3words: negotiators.ramp.eagles). Map ref. NGR 677155.

HILLFORTS OF SOMERSET

I am using the historical boundaries of 'greater' Somerset for this project, which makes it easier and less disjointed than using the unitary political districts of North Somerset and North-east Somerset, as well as the modern boundaries of the county of Somerset.

For this project, I am proposing that the tribal boundary to the south runs along the Mendip Hills, where a number of hillforts appear, beginning on the coast on the high ridge of Brean Down and running east to Dolebury Camp and Burrington Camp, both guarding north/south valleys through the Mendips at Churchill Gap and Burrington Combe, respectively.

The ground to the south of the Mendips is the beginning of the Somerset Levels, which 2500 years ago would have been a difficult, virtually impassable myriad of tidal swamps, islets and river channels. Perhaps Brent Knoll hillfort a few miles to the south of Brean Down was an isolated defended settlement, with sea access at that time, and was used as an outpost for the Dobunni. All speculation, but I have included this site as it is a good walk with spectacular views of the Mendips and the Levels, which gives an appreciation of the surrounding topography. The boundary continues east along the hills of north Somerset with Little Solsbury Hill overlooking the Avon valley.

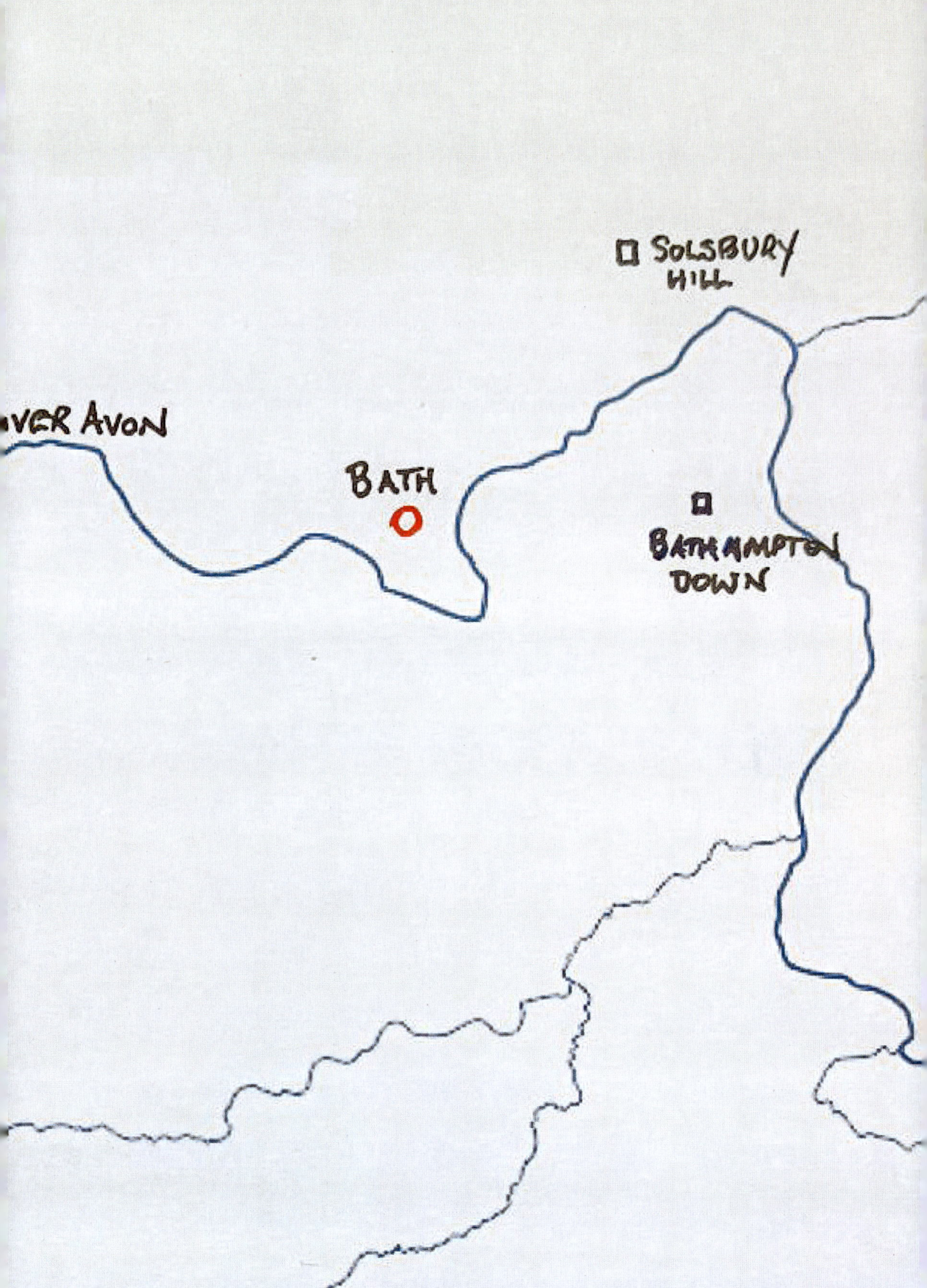

SOLSBURY
HILL
VER AVON
BATH
BATHAMPTON
DOWN

WORLEBURY CAMP

Sitting atop the limestone ridge of Worlebury Hill, overlooking Weston Bay to the south and Sand Bay to the north, is the stone-built, multivallate contour hillfort of Worlebury Camp. Steep cliffs drop down to the Bristol Channel to the north with steep to very steep slopes to the south and west. The interior of the fort measures 690m by 200m and encloses an area of 14ha.

The defences consist of tumbled stone ramparts, of which the inner three are still substantial, with four smaller ramparts beyond becoming increasingly smaller, each bank having an external ditch from which the building material was quarried. Originally the inner rampart was the largest,

being 10m wide with a height of 4m above the ditch bottom. The steep slopes/cliffs to the north provided adequate protection, but there may be remnants of a wall along the cliff edge. To the west and south where the slopes were less steep, there was a single rampart of stone 8m wide and 0.8m high.

There has been evidence found of hut platforms. A number of them have been found on the slopes; perhaps their purpose was a 'platform' for warfare. They are triangular in shape and 1.7m above the ground, with the apex flush with the hillside and the base projecting downhill, where ditches were dug in front of the platforms for defence. Sling stones have been found in the vicinity, suggesting slingers' platforms. Eighteen full skeletons from eighteen pits were discovered, ten of which had suffered a violent death, including sword cuts to the skull. This is a possible legacy from inter-tribal warfare or a possible stand against the ever-expanding Roman occupation of south-west Britain after the Claudian invasion of AD 43.

Excavations have found Neolithic and Bronze Age finds, including 36 flint chips, an arrowhead and a socketed bronze axe, suggesting early

Looking north over Worlebury Camp to Sand Bay and the Bristol Channel.

Looking south over the ramparts of Worlebury Camp to Weston Bay, with the pier in the background.

activity on the site. Storage pits have been found holding barley, wheat, peas, pottery and burnt woven baskets. Roman coins bearing the image of Honorius, who reigned from 393-423 AD (the Roman Emperor who refused help to the Romano-British as Britain was invaded by waves of Saxon and Pictish warriors, bringing an end to Roman interest in Britain in 410 AD), illustrates the length of time the site had seen human activity.

Parking is at the end of Worlebury Hill Road at the edge of the wood (what3words: manliness.ready.speech). A level walk of 3.5km extends along the top of the ridge; difficulty one. Landranger map 182. Map ref. NGR 314625.

BREAN DOWN CAMP

Located on the eastern end of the limestone ridge of Brean Down peninsula, this contour hillfort overlooks the sea at an elevation of 50m, with Weston Bay and Worlebury hillfort to the north and Berrow Flats to the south, looking down to Brent Knoll hillfort. The ridge is isolated from the Mendip Hills by the River Axe estuary, which enters the sea in Weston Bay.

The earthworks themselves have been extensively disturbed by quarrying, the construction of military buildings and the road which cuts through the ramparts east to west. As can be seen from the photo below the ramparts remaining visible are L-shaped with a stone bank and ditch running north to south across the ridge on the western side which is the

best preserved. To the south, the ramparts use the natural rock outcrop for its length to enhance the fort's defence.

Before quarrying work was carried out in the eighteenth and nineteenth centuries, the structure was described as square, and this, coupled with numerous Roman finds, suggested to historians at the time of Roman origin. However, following excavations (Burrow 1976), it was discovered with radiocarbon dating that the earthworks were constructed in the late Iron Age. As with many Iron Age hillforts, located as they were in prominent positions, the Romans later reused many of them for their own purposes, mainly as military strongholds and purpose-built legionary forts. Again, like many others this area, because of its location it has seen human activity from Neolithic times through to the 1940s and its Second World War military training uses. Excavated finds include Iron Age pottery, Roman pottery, gold coins and a ring.

Just for general interest: a directional concrete arrow (photograph below) is obvious from above, but not so much when walking. It is located on top of Brean Down, just along from the hillfort, and was constructed in the Second World War for the training of bomber pilots.

Brean Down is a National Trust Reserve with car parking at the base of the down (what3words: protected.charmingly.arranger). Numerous cafés and the wide expanse of the beach enhance the location. A round walk of 5km takes in the disused Victorian fort at the tip of the down. Difficulty four: a steep climb via steps or a gentler road climb is available: worth it for the views at the top. Landranger map 153. Map ref. NGR 285589.

BRENT KNOLL HILLFORT

Back in the Neolithic and Iron Age periods, Brent Knoll was an island hill standing at an elevation of 137m with 360-degree views of the Bristol Channel and the surrounding Somerset levels. Legend has it that the devil, when creating nearby Cheddar Gorge, threw a handful of rocks out towards the sea, and that became the Knoll. The Somerset levels are now well-drained agricultural land, but back then at high tide Brent Knoll would have been an isolated island; even at low tide it would have been surrounded by a myriad of bogs, pools and streams, a well-protected stronghold with the advantage of sea access.

Brent Knoll is a contour hillfort with a low rampart and an internal quarried ditch which circuits the summit edge of the flat top of the hill, enclosing an area of 1.6ha. There is then an external face which drops 2m to a step 2.75m wide, which then drops again to a wider outer terrace 4-6m wide, which may represent the remains of the outer ditch and counterscarp. The land then falls to the base of the slope.

The east entrance to the fort is a narrow hollow way (as seen in the next photo), leading up from the slope below. This was later used as a quarry track into the fort and the summit of the hill. The interior is much damaged from medieval quarrying, and from more recent times; the Second World War's Home Guard created slit trenches and a gun emplacement. There is evidence of Neolithic use, Bronze and Iron Age settlements and continuing use by the Romans, who built a temple on the summit and referred to the hill as the 'mount of frogs'. Excavations in the eighteenth and nineteenth centuries reference a hoard with coins from the eras of Roman emperors Trajan 98-117 AD and Severus 193-211 AD.

Parking is in the lane by St Michaels Church in the village of Brent Knoll (what3words: uncle.finger.major). The footpath leads up the hill from the right of the church. A walk of 2.5km, difficulty four, is worth the effort with the views of the Bristol Channel and the Somerset levels from the summit. Landranger map 182. Map ref. NGR 341509.

DOLEBURY CAMP, DOLEURY WARREN, ROWBERRY FORT

Dolebury Camp sits on top of the commanding east-west limestone ridge of Dolebury Warren on the north-west edge of the Mendip Hills. The Rowberry Fort, at an elevation of 183m, dominates the Churchill Gap, an ancient north-south route through the Mendip Hills. Because of the importance of the location, the site has been used throughout history from the Palaeolithic period to Roman times.

Looking east over Dolebury Camp, with the western entrance in the foreground and the surrounding steep slopes giving the fort its commanding position.

It is a univallate, partial contour fort comprising of a substantial single rampart 4m high and 12m wide with an outer ditch 10m wide and 1m deep, and counterscarp. On the southern side, the single rampart has a 5m-wide terrace below it, which then drops steeply to the valley below. The fort slopes downwards from east to west, with a height difference of some 30m; the interior is sub-rectangular in shape, measuring 487m by 200m, enclosing an area of 7ha.

In the seventeenth century, the interior of the fort was used as a huge artificial rabbit warren; evidence of this still remains with the presence of numerous pillow mounds (manmade low stone mounds covered in earth used as artificial rabbit warrens). Excavated finds include Palaeolithic flint work, Bronze Age pottery, a bronze spearhead, Roman coins and pottery. Three Roman coins found in the fort date from the emperors Gallienus (253-268 AD), Constantius II (352-354 AD) and Gratian (367-375 AD).

The western simple entrance through the single rampart, with the fort extending to the east, illustrating the change of elevation from east to west of some 30m.

The site is a scheduled ancient monument and a Site of Special Scientific Importance, owned by the National Trust and managed by the Avon Wildlife Trust.

Parking is at the Churchill village Memorial Hall, Ladymead Lane (what3words: supper.jaws.broached). Then cross the busy A38 and A368 and enter Jews Lane, which then becomes a footpath up through the woods. Walk 4km; difficulty four. Landranger map 193. Map ref. NGR 450589.

BURRINGTON CAMP

Burrington Camp sits above the steep-sided gorge of Burrington Combe on the north-western slope of Burrington Ham, a limestone plateau in the Mendip Hills. Combe, or Coombe, is of Celtic origin, denoting a steep-sided valley or hollow, which perfectly describes the gorge which defines Burrington Ham to the south and west. The slopes are precipitous to the south-west and north-west of the camp, less steep to the north-east and moderate to the east and south-east. In the below photo, taken from the north, the steep slopes of the Combe are visible just beyond the earthworks.

The camp is a univallate, hillslope fort defined by a single rampart 8m wide and 0.5m in height, and an outer ditch 3m wide and 0.5m deep.

Excavations carried out in 1960 (E.K. Tratman) showed the ramparts were of glacis/dump construction with a berm separating it from a flat-bottomed ditch. The site may be a two-phased construction with an initial L-shaped bank and ditch on the south and east side, as viewed from the south in the photo above. The second phase being to the north, west and a section of the south, comprising a smaller bank and an inner ditch instead of an outer one.

The camp (photo above), viewed from the north, with the precipitous slopes of the Combe to the west. An aerial view of the deeply incised Burrington Combe, again viewed from the north, can be seen at opposite.

The inner ditch may have ritual connotations, as Burrington Combe has seven caves located directly below the camp which could have religious connections. Burrington Combe is an important archaeological site; the cave of Avelines Hole contains the earliest dated human cemetery in Britain from 8400 years ago. A series of inscribed crosses found on the walls are believed to date from the early Mesolithic period, just after the Ice Age. Another cave within the Combe, Read's Cavern, contained Iron Age chariot gear, showing the area's significance during this period. Perhaps with the Combes caves and caverns providing the religious importance, the camp above was used for occasional rituals and feasting. The excavations of 1960 back this up, showing no evidence of permanent occupation of the camp.

The interior measures 75m by 100m, enclosing an area of 0.8ha; as we have seen, this area is too small to support a large settlement. With no evidence of occupation, not even a defended homestead, it leads to the idea of a livestock enclosure. This may be backed up with the evidence of

a segment of ditch on the north-west side which is divorced from the main enclosure, possibly part of an entrance and used to channel cattle into the enclosure.

Parking is in Burrington Combe near the caves (what3words: greet.collapsed.keys) or further on next to the nature reserve at Burrington Hamm car park (what3words: showering.vowing.reviewed). Both have an initial steep climb out of the Combe; difficulty four. From the nature reserve, it is a walk of 3.2km across the Ham. Landranger map 182. Map ref. NGR 478587.

CADBURY CAMP, TICKENHAM

This is one of three hillforts in Somerset named 'Cadbury', the others being Cadbury Castle, South Cadbury in south Somerset and Cadbury Hill Camp, near Congresbury. Located on the eastern end of a ridge with an elevation of 110m separating the Gordano Valley and the Somerset Levels is the small sub-circular, bivallate, partial contour fort of Cadbury Camp, which encloses an area of 2.7ha. In its prominent position, the view to the south-west takes in Worlebury Camp and the Bristol Channel, and south to Dolebury Warren, sitting high up on the Mendip Hills.

The camp angles down to the east with steep surrounding slopes to the north, south and east; less so along the ridge to the west. The earthworks

comprise two ramparts and ditches; the internal bank is 2m high, with the medial ditch 2m deep. The external bank stands 1.5m high with an outer ditch 2m deep. Excavations (H. St George Gray 1922) were carried out within the camp, along with the ramparts being sectioned where it was discovered that they were constructed of small stones quarried from the ditches. There are three current entrances, two of which are modern, but the one facing north is thought to be the original elaborate entrance.

The excavations indicate Iron Age occupation, with late Romano-British continuation or reuse. Finds include Neolithic flints and a Bronze Age spearhead (found in 1856 and now held in the Museum of Somerset in Taunton). Substantial Roman activity on the site is illustrated with evidence of late Roman coins from the reigns of Claudius II (Claudius-Gothicus 268-

270 AD) and Valentinian II (375-387 AD). The site was damaged during the Second World War when it was used by a searchlight battery and also used for bomb disposal.

The area is jointly managed by the National Trust and Natural England. Parking is at Tickenham village hall (what3words: cherry.colleague.bucks); parking fees are paid online via a smartphone, there is no cash alternative available. The footpath, which heads straight up the hill, is found 100m left of the car park. The walk is 2.5km, with a difficulty of four, but the effort is worth it for the views, as well as checking out the hillfort.

MAES KNOLL CAMP

Located on the eastern end of Dundry Hill ridge at an elevation of 197m, overlooking the urban sprawl of south Bristol, is the prominent, univallate, partial contour fort of Maes Knoll Camp. The camp is semi-triangular in shape and encloses 10.5ha; the shape of the earthworks depend on the topography, following the contours around the flat-topped ridge.

There are steep surrounding slopes to the north, south and east, moderate to level along the ridge to the north-west of the camp, which is dominated by a massive cross bank and rock-cut ditch measuring 61m in length that cuts off the access from the ridge. Locally known as 'the tump',

base of the ditch. The defences are slighter and generally depend on the steepness of the surrounding natural scarps; only traces on the north and south sides of a single bank and rock-cut ditch are left after being ploughed down over the millennia. A possible original entrance is located between the north end of the tump and the scarp, though this may have been enlarged in modern times.

The name 'Maes Knoll' is derived from the Brythonic word 'Maes', meaning 'flat top', and the Old English 'Knoll' or 'Knowle', meaning hill. The camp is considered Iron Age, possibly constructed around 250 BC and modified later in the post-Roman period to form the western end of the Wansdyke. Excavated finds include Iron Age pottery found near the north-west entrance (P.A.Rahtz 1958). Pottery, two worked flints and a whetstone were found at the eastern end of the camp.

The area was used during the Second World War with a hut being built on the top of the tump for the local Home Guard to use as a lookout post to give early warning of enemy aircraft and potential parachute and or glider landings on the flat-topped ridge. Stone cairns were built on top of the ridge to help deter enemy glider landings; though long gone now, they were still prominent for many post-war years.

On-road parking is at the north end of Church Road, Norton Malreward (what3words: nuns.digit.pool). The footpath leads straight up to Maes Knoll from the road; the walk is 2.6km; difficulty four. The views at the top of the ridge are spectacular, with views towards the Avon Valley, Bath and Solsbury Hill to the east, the Mendip Hills to the south, and looking north and west over Bristol and the Clifton suspension bridge standing above the Avon Gorge.

LITTLE SOLSBURY HILL CAMP

Solsbury Hill occupies a commanding position on the summit of a prominent hill standing at 191m overlooking a major south-east bend of the River Avon and the city of Bath below. It is a univallate contour hillfort which is roughly triangular in shape, enclosing a relatively flat interior of 7.9ha. Steep slopes surround the fort, south, west and east, with a more moderate slope to the north-west where the original in-turned entrance is located.

The single stone-faced rampart was up to 4m in height and some 6m in width, but nowadays measures just 0.9m high around the contour edge. Apart from just below the north rampart where the ditch is just visible,

and the southern side, where there is a shallow 0.5-1m-deep ditch with counterscarp, it seems the steep slopes east and west may have provided enough protection with the high rampart topping the escarpment, or maybe the final construction was never finished.

Excavations in 1955, 1956 and 1958 by W.A. Dowden revealed timber hut circles dated to the first Iron Age with rampart construction about 300 BC, later replaced by stone hut circles, about 150 BC. It seems the main occupation of the site was in the second century BC, with it being abandoned sometime between 100-50 BC before the Roman period.

Finds include flint implements, leaf-shaped flint arrowheads, scrapers and worked bone and horn. With later Iron Age artefacts, much excavated burnt clay and charcoal is evidence of bloomery metal working.

Parking is off the A46 on a side road (what3words: beast.royal.kicked). The footpath heads north up a private road then climbs back towards the south up to Solsbury Hill; length of walk 2.5km; difficulty two/three. Landranger map 172. Map ref. NGR 768679.

HILLFORTS OF WILTSHIRE

Wiltshire is a large county with rich links to archaeological sites of pre-history, the most famous being the ancient ceremonial landscape containing Stonehenge. There is a wide and varied mix of sites, including causewayed enclosures, the large stone circle at Avebury Henge (which pre-dates Stonehenge and is a larger monument), barrows, Cursuses and hillforts. Here, we focus on the northern half of the county, where a line of hillforts extends west to east along the chalk uplands of the northern edge of the Vale of Pewsey. From the west, we begin with Olivers Castle, standing above the town of Devizes; Rybury Castle; Giants Grave and Martinsell Camp; then continue in a north-easterly direction to the spectacular hillforts of Barbury and Liddington.

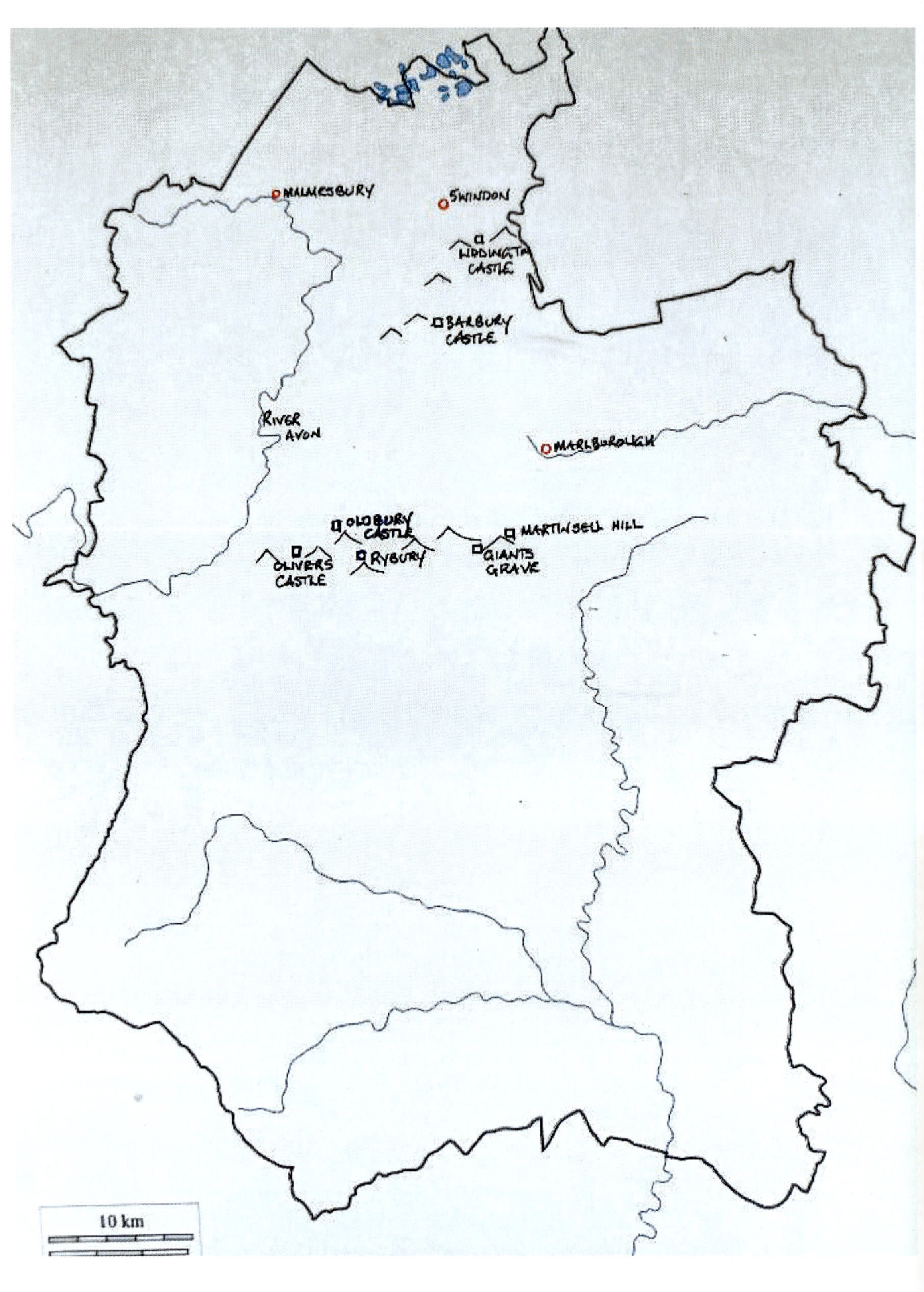
MALMESBURY
SWINDON
LIDDINGTON CASTLE
BARBURY CASTLE
RIVER AVON
MARLBOROUGH
OLDBURY CASTLE
MARTINSELL HILL
OLIVERS CASTLE
RYBURY
GIANTS GRAVE
10 km

OLIVER'S CASTLE

Roughly triangular in shape, this promontory hillfort is located on an east-west spur of the chalk uplands of Roundway Down, and at an elevation of 209m, overlooks the western end of the Vale of Pewsey. There are steep natural slopes to the north, west and south, with a single bank and ditch cutting off the promontory to the level plateau to the east. The in-filled ditch, which now appears as a berm/terrace below the rampart, is now a trackway which surrounds the earthworks. There is a single entrance to the east, following excavations by B.H. and M.E. Cunnington in 1907; this entrance was probably gated.

Although small, the earthworks enclose an area of 1.3ha. The geographic position of the fort with commanding views allows control of the resources below in the Vale of Pewsey. There is little evidence of a permanent occupation of the site and it has been referred to as an 'empty' hillfort; this

was backed up by a geophysics study (Payne 2006) which found little or no evidence of hut circles or storage pits.

Was the site, because of its commanding position, used as a lookout station for observing the valley below, the rolling hills of Salisbury Plain on the horizon to the south and neighbouring tribal land? Or was it used for ceremonial purposes and occasional feasting and celebration rituals at certain religious times of the year (there are two barrows on the south-western tip of the promontory)? It may have been used as a place of safety for the local inhabitants, or maybe all three or none of these reasons. Excavations have uncovered Bronze Age, Iron Age and Romano-British pottery shards, which show the extent of the use of the fort for whatever reason from about 600 BC onwards.

The name given to the hillfort is associated with the English civil war Battle of Roundway Down, fought in 1643. Fleeing Parliamentary cavalry who were escaping from a Royalist charge were forced to gallop over the

91m-high precipice at the edge of Roundway Down near the hillfort; many died at the foot of the hill, and the area became known locally as 'Bloody Ditch'. From this action, the hillfort became known as Oliver's Castle, even though Oliver Cromwell was not present at the battle.

Heading east out of Devizes on the London Road, turn left at the Travel Lodge and head up a steep single-track lane. Fork right and parking is found overlooking the White Horse (what3words: jogging.videos.snack). The footpath runs along the edge of Roundway Down through the woods, and the walk is 5km; difficulty two. Landranger map 173. Map ref. NGR 001646.

OLDBURY CASTLE

The nineteenth-century antiquarian Sir Richard Colt Hoare said of Oldbury Castle: 'the fort is very irregular, humouring the hill in its numerous sinuosities'. This is an accurate view of what is a complex set of earthworks located on the chalk uplands on the summit of Cherhill Hill, where the natural topography has dictated the layout of the fort, which is not flat and varies up to 23m in height. Roughly triangular in shape, enclosing an area of 8ha, Oldbury Castle is bivallate, apart from the north side where a single, low bank is found on the summit edge of the steep escarpment. It is a partial contour fort, with ramparts and ditches extending down the west side of the

entrance which is protected by the outer bank or barbican.

The interior of the fort is bisected by a north-west to south-east bank following the edge of the plateau, which may represent a boundary ditch pre-dating the hillfort construction. Following a geophysical survey in 1996, a ditch was discovered which extends from the north side of the east

entrance to a point halfway along the northern rampart, dated to the late Bronze Age, which may again be a linear boundary ditch or field boundary.

Flint digging and chalk quarrying have affected much of the interior to the west and south. Excavations have uncovered late Bronze Age, Iron Age and Romano-British pottery, quern stones and Roman coins from the reigns of Domitian (81-96 AD) and Magnus Maximus (383-388 AD).

North of the fort on the escarpment is the Cherhill White Horse, cut in 1780 by Dr. Christopher Allsop of Calne. Standing at the north-west corner of the fort is the Cherhill or Lansdowne Monument, an obelisk built in 1845, standing at 38m high and designed by Sir Charles Barry, the architect responsible for the rebuilding of the Palace of Westminster.

There are lay-bys along the A4 for parking (what3words: install. swordfish.allowable). The walk is 3km, with a quite steep walk up the chalk escarpment: difficulty three. Landranger map 173. Map ref. NGR 049693.

RYBURY CAMP

Overlying an existing Neolithic causewayed enclosure on the spur of the summit of Rybury Hill is Rybury Camp, a small contour hillfort offering amazing views of Pewsey Vale and the rolling chalk uplands; again, a potentially strategic control point over the valley below. The earthworks comprise a bank and ditch which is 1.5m deep with a counterscarp bank standing 1.1m above the ditch, enclosing an area of 1.4ha. A trench examined in 1963 by Desmond Bonney revealed the ditch was originally flat-bottomed and 2.1m deep. The camp is surrounded by steep slopes, apart from the south-east, where a col exists between it and its sister, Clifford's Hill; both stand at over 240m.

As can be seen in the below photograph, the interior of the camp is pockmarked with post-medieval chalk and flint quarrying pits; excavations

have uncovered 600 flint flakes on site, showing the site was used to fashion tools. A simple entrance is located on the southern side of the ramparts which opens onto the col; this is probably original.

The camp has been dated to the late Bronze Age to early Iron Age. To the north 1km, running east-west along the ridge of Tan Hill, is the Wansdyke, a 35-mile (56km)-long ditch and earthwork bank built in the years following the Roman evacuation of Britain as a defensive barrier against West Saxon incursions.

Parking is available at a couple of small off-road locations (what3words: stammer.drawn.incorrect; companies.caged.hamster; reception.storm.flushes). The walk is 4.5km, difficulty three, but again well worth the effort for the views alone. Landranger map 174. Map ref. NGR 083639.

MARTINSELL CAMP

Situated on top of Martinsell Hill, a steep downland spur, jutting out into the Vale of Pewsey, standing at 289m, is Martinsell Camp, the highest pre-historic camp in Wiltshire, the second-highest point on Pewsey Downs, and the third-highest point in Wiltshire. Rectangular in shape, the camp is a univallate, partial contour fort enclosing an area of 13ha. The single rampart is up to 3.2m in height with the outer ditch 1m deep. However, the ditch to the east fades to a terrace and boundary bank, and the north-west has been much destroyed by quarrying. There are multiple modern breaks in the ramparts, but those at the north-east and south-west are possibly original.

Given the camp's geographic position—high up, strategically overlooking and potentially controlling the eastern end of the Vale of Pewsey—a geophysical survey carried out (Payne 2006) found evidence of little activity within the fort. Mark Bowden (2005) describes the camp as a 'hilltop enclosure', suggesting that it may have been a defended settlement and used for livestock. But considering its position and defensive earthworks in its earliest form, this was, again, I believe a Dobunnic frontier fort overlooking Salisbury Plain to the south and guarding the Vale of Pewsey from the potential threats posed from neighbouring tribes.

Numerous chance finds within the fort and nearby include Iron Age stamped, incised and finger-decorated pottery and Roman sherds, including first- and second-century Samian and Savernake wares. Coins found nearby

belong to the reign of Cunobelin, the pre-Roman King of the Catuvellauni tribe 9-40 AD, and his brother, Epaticcus.

Along the ridge 800m to the south-west is another hillfort, Giant's Grave; this is a possible inland promontory fort located on a steep-sided spur standing 250m above the Vale of Pewsey. The site is protected by a single bank and ditch cutting off the promontory north-west to south-east, enclosing an area of 1 ha. The bank averages 3m in height and is 18m wide, with the ditch on the east side 10m wide. There is evidence of an outer bank 2.2m high with a ditch 0.6m deep, but it has an unfinished appearance. The traditional view that Giant's Grave is an inland promontory fort has been challenged by Mark Bowden (2005), who suggests that the site is a section of a series of earthworks making up a massive cross-ridge dyke restricting

Giant's Grave, promontory fort or enclosed farmstead; whatever it is, it is a lovely spot to take in the views of Pewsey Vale.

access from the east. Discussions have taken place about the use of this site, chiefly because of its small size. Was it part of or associated with the larger fort of Martinsell Camp, or does it date to an earlier time?

There is a car park on Martinsell Hill (what3words: waggled.baker.nurture). The walk taking in both sites is 4.5km; difficulty three. Landranger map 173. Map ref. NGR 189582.

BARBURY CASTLE

In a commanding position standing at 262m on the west end of a west-facing promontory on Barbury Down is the massive, bivallate contour hillfort of Barbury Castle. Located just south of the ancient Ridgeway and at the north end of the River Og valley, the two concentric rings of banks and ditches enclose an area of 4.5ha.

The inner bank is 10m wide and has a level rampart top of 5m wide and stands up to 3m high measured from the interior. There is a substantial inner ditch 24m wide, constructed by digging into the natural slope and building up the rampart, which is 10m above the base of the ditch. The

outer rampart is 15m wide, has a 7.5m-wide level top and is 3.5m high. The outer ditch is narrower at 10m wide and 3m deep.

There are two original entrances facing out to east and west. The western entrance was widened during the Second World War when the War Ministry appropriated the site for the U.S. Army to use as an anti-aircraft gun emplacement to allow trucks and guns into the interior. There is evidence still of slit trenches, and bases for the guns are visible as hollows around the edge of the interior of the fort.

A number of Bronze Age burial mounds can be seen from the fort in the immediate area, indicating that Barbury was a significant place even before the fort began to be constructed around 700 BC. In 1996, a geophysical survey revealed traces of forty hut circles and many pits, often used for storage of grain and other foodstuffs during times of plenty, suggesting the site had a long period of occupation. Surface finds include Iron Age and Roman pottery, as well as Iron Age jewellery and chariot fittings found within the interior.

The site is found within Barbury Castle Country Park where there is a car park (what3words: issues.modest.plants), toilets and ongoing discussions around having a café on site. The walk is 3km taking in a circuit of the ramparts, difficulty one, on quite level ground.

LIDDINGTON CASTLE

This is a strategically sited univallate contour hillfort on an exposed position on the north chalk downland plateau edge of Liddington Hill, with views north and west across the Thames Valley and south to the Marlborough Downs. The fort is surrounded by exposed steep slopes and is located just north of the ancient track of the Ridgeway.

Roughly oval in shape, the fort comprises an inner bank 12m wide and standing up to 3m above the interior. The ditch is 18m wide with a substantial counterscarp, with the inner bank rising to 6m above the bottom of the ditch. Small-scale excavations carried out in 1976 discovered the ramparts were constructed in at least four phases. The earliest was between the

eighth and seventh centuries BC, and the last phase showed refortification in the Saxon period. The original rampart was reveted with timber at the rear, succeeded by two phases of glacis/dump construction of chalk rubble, with a possible front revetment of chalk sarsens. If this was the case, it was a statement of dominance for the local chieftain and his aristocracy, for the white chalk ramparts would have been visible for miles across the Thames Valley up to the oppida at Bagendon some 24 miles (39 km) to the north.

There is a simple causewayed entrance on the south-east side which is the most accessible. It is 3m wide, with several sarsen stones visible at the base of the rampart terminals; these may have been used to face the entrance. There was an original entrance on the south-west side, but it was blocked off and is visible as a wide, topped section of rampart between two enlarged terminals. A geophysical survey showed a large 18m-diameter round house and numerous storage pits in the interior. Flint digging carried

out in the north-east interior between 1896-1900 led to an excavation of Iron Age artefacts including a bronze awl, a bronze ear ring, saddle quern fragments and spindle whorls. Finds in more recent times span from the Mesolithic (a perforated quartzite pebble) to the Anglo-Saxon period (a spear head).

Liddington Castle has been put forwards as a possible site for the battle of Mount Badon c. 500 AD, where a resounding British victory led by the legendary King Arthur halted the westwards expansion of the Anglo-Saxons for a generation. Historians Michael Wood and Kate Prendergast have both suggested this site because of its strategic position on the ancient Ridgeway and adjacent to Ermin Way, the Roman road connecting Silchester to Gloucester via Swindon and Cirencester. However, following excavations by Hirst and Rahtz in 1996 to link Liddington Castle to the battle of Mount Badon, no evidence was found to confirm whether it had taken place in or around the fort.

Parking is in a lay-by off the Ridgeway (what3words: radiated.latest.timer) or off the B4192, just where the Ridgeway bridle path starts climbing Liddington Hill (what3words: eventful.walked.punctual). The walk is 3.7km; difficulty three. Landranger map 174. Map ref. NGR 209797.

HILLFORTS OF OXFORDSHIRE

The chalk uplands continue in an easterly direction from Liddington Castle into the rolling hills of Oxfordshire, where the fortifications continue eastwards with Hardwell Camp and Uffington Castle, east to Segsbury Camp, Blewbury Hill and Sinodun Hill. These sites border the River Thames, which forms a section of the eastern boundary. To the north, the countryside is more rolling, but there are earthworks at Lyneham Camp, Knollbury and Chastleton, again, which border the River Cherwell which continues the eastern boundary in a northerly direction.

6 mi
CHASTLETON CAMP
KNOLLBURY CAMP
RIVER CHERWELL
OXFORD
CHERBURY CAMP
RIVER THAMES
SINODUN HILL
HARDWELL CASTLE
UFFINGTON CASTLE
SEGSBURY
BLEWBURTON HILL

UFFINGTON CASTLE AND WHITE HORSE

In a prominent position on White Horse Hill, overlooking the Vale of the White Horse to the north and the Berkshire Downs to the south, is the impressive contour hillfort of Uffington Castle. It comprises a D-shaped enclosure of 3.2ha, univallate with a ditch and counterscarp for its entire circuit. The rampart is 12m wide and stands 2.5m above the interior of the fort; the ditch is V-shaped, 15m wide and measures 3m from the bottom to the top of the rampart. The counterscarp is 8m wide and 1m in height.

As can be seen in the photograph above, the original entrance is on the west-facing rampart consisting of out-turned links and an enlarged counterscarp bank to the front. There is a blocked entrance to the east; it was originally a passageway containing guard chambers. The two breaks in the rampart to the north-east and south-east are possibly Romano-British.

A geophysical survey (Miles 2003) and following excavations revealed pits, postholes and rectangular features within the interior of the fort. Dobunnic coins were found nearby, perhaps reinforcing the idea that

Uffington was within that sphere of influence. The rampart construction was dated to two phases, with the initial comprising a timber box rampart from the eighth to seventh centuries BC, followed by a glacis/dump rampart in the fourth century BC.

The famous White Horse is the oldest chalk cut figure in Britain, perhaps over 3000 years old. Nearby Dragon Hill, a natural mound 10m high, is named after its association with the legend of St George. The hill has an artificially flattened top with a bare patch of chalk upon which no grass will grow and is purported to be where the dragon's blood flowed. There

are suggestions that the mound was an Iron Age ritual site associated with the chalk cut figure above it.

Parking is at the National Trust car park (what3words: wimp.extension.tonight). An uphill walk of 3.4km includes Dragon Hill; difficulty three. Landranger map 173. Map ref. NGR 189582.

HARDWELL CAMP

Located about 1km west of Uffington Castle, also on the north-facing chalk uplands, but not on the highest ground, is Hardwell Camp, standing at 182m, some 80m below Uffington in an overlooked position. Clearly this is not a strategic setting; using ramparts, ditches and natural slopes, the site is complex and difficult to interpret, but does use the natural topography to great advantage. As seen from the photograph below, the site is triangular in shape with two small but deeply incised valleys that run from the southern base of the triangle down the slope to the northern apex. The northern rampart runs along the top edge of the small valleys; built of stone rubble and

turf, it measures 10m wide and stands between 0.5m and 1.5m above the interior. Ramparts follow the inside top edges of both the east and west valleys. Across the relatively flat ground to the south, this more-open side is protected running east to west by an inner bank 10m wide and 2.5m high, with an outer ditch 16m wide and 1-2m deep, with an outer bank with similar dimensions to the inner one. The original entrance is in the south side, possibly a corridor with outworks, further protected by an outer bank. There is a possible north entrance which is a simple gap in the rampart leading down the scarp face.

Natural valleys provide natural defence to Hardwell Camp. The first photo (below) looking south is of the eastern valley, which from the base to the top of the rampart to the right is some 15m in height. The valley on the west side is not so deep, but at 6-7m, is still a formidable natural barrier; even more so if you can picture the original rampart along the top edge.

There is no specific parking for Hardwell Camp, but the National Trust car park for Uffington Castle can be used (what3words: wimp.extension.tonight). For the walk, follow the Ridgeway path just to the south of Uffington Castle to the west, and then a footpath leads down the slope, with Hardwell Camp on the right. The site is covered with dense woodland. Be aware it is currently used for pheasant rearing. The walk is 5km; difficulty three. Landranger map 173. Map ref. NGR 287866.

BLEWBURTON HILL

The earthworks follow the contours of the isolated Blewburton Hill, standing at 110m above the flat surrounding Oxfordshire countryside, and enclosing an area of 4.1ha. As previously mentioned when discussing wooden palisades, the hillfort was originally univallate, but has been interpreted to have a three-phase construction. Originally a stockaded camp in the sixth or seventh century BC, this then developed to a timber boxed rampart in the sixth or fifth century BC; then further dump ramparts and ditches were added in the second or first century BC. The fort seems to have been abandoned in the first century BC. The western entrance, as shown in the photograph below, has been excavated and has been shown to have been built

in three phases. Originally it had a cobbled surface with a timber reveted passageway, which was replaced by a stone lined entrance; unusually, evidence of horse burials were discovered in the inner passageway.

The above photograph is looking north over the fort towards Wittenham Clumps, just visible on the horizon.

Road parking is in Bessels Lea, Blewbury (what3words: doubts.lush.hobbyists). The footpath with farm buildings to your left heads due east; the earthworks reveal themselves as you approach steadily uphill. The walk is 2.5km; difficulty two. Landranger map 174. Map ref. NGR 547862.

SINODUN CAMP, WITTENHAM CLUMPS, CASTLE HILL

The two prominent wooded chalk hills known locally as 'the Clumps' mark the farthest east of the hillforts of the Dobunnic tribal region. The River Thames is less than 500m to the north and then flows south, marking the frontier. In the below photograph the Thames is visible in the background with 'the Clumps' to the fore. Round Hill to the north, standing at 120m, is higher than the southern clump, which is called Castle or Sinodun Hill; the name 'Sinodun' is pure

Celtic, meaning 'old fort'. Standing at 107m above the Thames Valley, it offers views northwards up the Thames Valley and to the south and west across the Vale of the White Horse to the Berkshire Downs, where we have seen a series of hillforts follow the line of the ancient Ridgeway.

Sinodun Camp is a univallate contour hillfort comprising a rampart, ditch and a substantial counterscarp for the entire circuit. The earthworks enclose an area of 4.5ha. There are two possible original entrances: a simple one to the south-west with possible outworks and one to the north-east, which was in-turned.

A geophysics survey by English Heritage revealed an inner buried ditch forming an enclosure in the middle of the interior of the fort, which was dated to the late Bronze Age. Allen carried out further geophysical surveys in 2010, which showed the fort's construction and occupation from the early/mid Iron Age; it was abandoned in the late Iron Age then reused by the late Romano-British, and was further occupied medievally. The Time Team Project spent three days researching and excavating the southern slopes of Round Hill in 2004 where evidence of a Romano-British house was uncovered, complete with a mosaic floor and painted wall plaster. Excavated finds from the area include an oval bronze shield, 35cm in diameter, retrieved from the nearby River Isis in 1836. Also found in 1982 was the famous Wittenham Sword and scabbard, dating from the late Iron Age (120 BC–43 AD).

The grassed slopes of both hills lead up to the oldest beech tree plantings in Britain, dating to the 1740s. The site is owned by the Earth Trust, which manages the site as a nature reserve. Car parking is available (what3words: global.feed.sprinkler). The walk is 2km if taking in both hills; difficulty two. Landranger map 164. Map ref. NGR 569924.

CHERBURY CAMP

Cherbury Camp comes under the rare classification of marsh fort and was constructed on a dry tongue of land surrounded by wet marshy ground. The area has now been drained and is a rich agricultural landscape, but in Iron Age times, this area was low-lying marsh bordering the River Thames some 2km to the north.

The fort is a bivallate and its oval shape encloses an area of 4.6ha; the earthworks comprise two ramparts and ditches with a counterscarp, though much denuded, to the east. The original entrance to the east following excavations (Bradford 1940) was shown to be in-turned, with dry stone revetting which carried on along the outer face of the inner rampart.

Aerial photography and a geophysical survey (Wintle 2009) showed evidence of round houses and storage pits. Pottery from excavations and subsequent surface collection (Hingly 1983) is dated to the early/mid Iron Age period.

Park in the village of Charney Basset on the road outside St Peters church (what3words: debate.continues.initiates). There is a footpath leading to the fort north of the village; 5.5 km walk; difficulty one. Landranger map 164. Map ref. NGR 374963.

OTHER HILLFORTS OF OXFORDSHIRE

Badbury Hill/Camp, photographed below, is a univallate, roughly circular contour hillfort located on a slight hill overlooking the Vale of the White Horse to the south with Uffington Castle on the far horizon. The site is heavily wooded, with the bank and ditch visible for much of the circuit. The area is managed by the National Trust, with the car park adjacent to the camp (what3words: herds.spoiler.grapevine). The length of the walk is less than 1km around the perimeter of the earthworks, but can be extended with signposted circular walks through the woods. Landranger map 170. Map ref. NGR 262946.

To the north of the county, in the rolling hills around Chipping Norton, are a number of other hillforts, one of which is Knollbury Camp; however, it is on private land with no public access. The above photograph is of the hillslope fort of Knollbury Camp, a rectilinear univallate earthwork enclosing an area of 1.4ha, lying just to the north of the village of Chadlington and adjacent to farmland belonging to TV celebrity Jeremy Clarkson. The single rampart measures 10m wide and ranges from 1.5–4m in height. The defensive quarry ditch, which has been largely filled in from years of cultivation, would have measured 10m wide. The gaps seen in the ramparts are modern; there have been no excavations, but evidence from geophysical surveys suggest possible Roman reuse. The earthworks do resemble a Roman legionary fort, but there is no evidence to support that this was a later structure constructed post AD 43.

The site is on private land but can be viewed from the adjacent road (what3words: storage.utensil.slot). Landranger map 164. Map ref. NGR 316230.

Below is a photograph of Chastleton Camp, located some 6km west of Chipping Norton. Situated on top of Chastleton Hill at a height of 239m, this univallate feature enclosing 1.4ha was, I suggest, too small for a large settlement, and may have been a defended farmstead for an extended family and its livestock. The bank is 14m wide and stands between 2-4m in height. There is no evidence of a ditch (Lang 2009), although there are suggestions of one on the east side which may have been 14m wide. A tree line now covers the bank, which has damaged and degraded it to some degree.

Parking is on either side of the nearby road (what3words: hothouse. towns.boast). There is a footpath which runs through the camp, accessed from the road leading to the adjacent farm. The area is popular with dog walkers, and on the opposite side of the road from the camp is a large field with a circular walk taking in the views of the rolling hills looking westwards towards Stow on the Wold. Landranger map 163. Map ref. NGR 259282.

HILLFORTS OF (SOUTH) WORCESTERSHIRE

The Dobunnic sphere of influence extended into modern-day south Worcestershire, specifically Bredon Hill, which had three hillforts located on its west-, north- and southern-facing slopes. Bredon Hill is geologically part of the Cotswolds and lies within the Cotswolds Area of Outstanding Natural Beauty. However, due to natural causes, it now stands isolated in the Vale of Evesham. With the River Isbourne to the east and the River Avon flowing around the north and west of the hill, along with the River Severn to the west, Bredon Hill strategically dominates the flat floodplains surrounding it.

KEMERTON CAMP

Located at the north-west end of Bredon Hill is the multivallate, promontory hillfort of Kemerton Camp. Two ramparts cut off the triangular-shaped promontory enclosing an area of 7.1ha, with precipitous slopes to the north and west providing natural protection to the site. The outer bank is 13.5m wide and 2.4m high, with a V-shaped rock-cut ditch 10m wide and 4.5m deep. The inner bank is of glacis construction, measuring 33m wide and standing up to 11m high above the V-shaped ditch with a possible timber breastwork. The original entrance is found in the south-west corner; excavations have shown it to have a phased construction. A simple entrance was

made in phase one. It was made more complex in phase two, with a 40m-passageway with revetted walls between in-turns, with evidence of a timber bridge above. Phase three was the addition of two further entrances at the rampart ends near the cliffs.

Kemerton Camp is believed to have been abandoned sometime in the first century AD. Initially, the view held by historians was that this occurred following a siege by Roman forces expanding westwards. The mutilated remains of sixty adult male skeletons were excavated (Hencken 1938) outside the inner gate, along with weapons and burnt material indicating a fierce struggle, which backed up the Roman siege theory. However, the skeletons found in the entrance have been carbon-14 dated (Hurst and Weston 2012) to between 170–50 BC, so were possibly the result of inter-tribal warfare and not following resistance to the Claudian Roman invasion some 100 years or more later. Other finds include a fluted spearhead of

similar Continental European design of the second century BC, Iron Age pottery, weapons, metal work and human and animal bone fragments.

A stone tower called Parsons' Folly or the Banbury Stone Tower is found on the inner rampart, where it ends above the west-facing cliff line. It is named after John Parsons MP (1732-1805), who had the tower built as a summer house offering views of the Severn Valley southwards and the Malvern Hills to the west. There are a number of standing stones found in the interior of the fort. The 'Banbury Stone', deriving its name from the eighth century name for the fort, 'Baenintesburg', is known locally as the 'elephant stone' because of its resemblance to the creature. Another pair of stones are known as the 'King and Queen Stones' and local legend say that if you pass between them, you will be cured of illness.

Parking is in Elmley Castle village at a small car park opposite the cricket pitch (what3words: alarming.maps.poetry). A walk taking in all three hillforts on Bredon Hill is 11km, difficulty four. Landranger map 150. Map ref. NGR 957401.

CONDERTON CAMP

Located on the south-facing spur at the eastern end of Bredon Hill, with extensive views down the Severn Valley, is the univallate, hillslope fort of Conderton Camp. Built in two phases, carbon-14 dating (Horn Forthcoming) pottery found on site suggests phase one construction began between 520-400 BC, comprising a rampart and ditch with counterscarp enclosing an area of 1.95ha with a simple gap/entrance facing north and one to the south overlooking a spring. During phase two, occurring between 400-260 BC, the southern rampart was pulled back to form a more rectilinear enclosure with a smaller

footprint of 0.71ha. This new rampart had no ditch but a central in-turned entrance with possibly a timber framed gate. So why the change in the layout?

Was there a time of strife and inter-tribal warfare in the region? The dates of phase two at Conderton do not tie in with the excavated skeletal finds following a fierce battle at nearby Kemerton Camp; it pre-dates that possible date by at least 100 years. Possibly the strategic position of Bredon Hill and its hillforts made it a region ripe for conquest and warfare from covetous neighbours throughout the Iron Age period.

Although now smaller in size, this new enclosure was crammed with huts, storage pits and other structures on a planned basis. The stone-lined pits, numbering 140, were to the west side, and ten stone-built circular structures were to the east, along with circular platforms sited just inside

the rampart on the southern entrance, possibly guard huts. The earlier constructed south section of the enclosure is free of any structures and pits and may have been used as a livestock enclosure. The hillfort was abandoned between 200–125 BC, though possibly reused as a defended homestead through to the Romano-British period.

Rich in excavated finds, Conderton Camp provided loom weights, copper alloy rings, iron objects, plough tips, nails, spindle whorls and saddle querns. Roman coins from the reign of Trajan (98–117 AD) and Constantine (306–37 AD) were found, possibly showing later use.

Parking is for Kemerton Camp, for a longer walk visiting all three hillforts on Bredon Hill. Alternatively, for a shorter walk, park by the Yew Tree pub in the village of Conderton (what3words: playful.removers.throw). The walk is straight up Pigeon Lane, 3km, difficulty two/three. Landranger map 150. Map ref. NGR 972384.

ELMLEY CASTLE

Sited on a prominent spur on the north-east facing slopes of Bredon Hill is Elmley Castle; it is possibly two Iron Age hillforts or one constructed in two phases. The exact form of the Iron Age defences are difficult to disentangle from the later Norman Motte and Bailey built within the earthworks and the later medieval castle. The Iron Age ramparts provide the outer rampart, ditch and counterscarp, which are well preserved to the north, south and east; however, the southern rampart may be a Norman re-cutting of the original earthwork. The large inner Bailey is Norman and is commanding over the northern slope leading down to the village of Elmley Castle.

A stone castle existed from Norman times, originally built by Robert Le Despenser; following his death and by marriage, the castle passed to the

Beauchamp family, Earls of Warwick who used Elmley Castle as a secondary possession after Warwick Castle. By 1544, the castle was in a state of decay, with the stone being carried away for use in the building and maintaining of nearby Pershore Bridge. The surrounding land is the former medieval deer park belonging to the castle. However, the site is on private land and there are no footpaths or public access to the castle. The nearest footpath runs down the slope to the east of the site.

Parking is in Elmley Castle village, as for Kemerton Camp (what3words: alarming.maps.poetry). Landranger map 150. Map ref. NGR 979402.

HILLFORTS OF HEREFORDSHIRE

West of Bredon Hill and across the River Severn lies the county of Herefordshire, the north-west region of the Dobunni tribe. The county is rich in hillforts providing some of the largest earthworks in Britain at Credenhill Camp and the spectacular contour hillfort of British Camp sitting atop Herefordshire Beacon in the Malvern Hills. The region is bounded by the River Wye to the west and the river Teme to the east and north.

BRANDON CAMP
RIVER TEME
WAPLEY HILL
BURFA BANK
CROFT AMBREY
RIVER LUGG
RIVER WYE
CREDENHILL CAMP
SUTTON WALLS
BRITISH CAMP
MIDSUMMER HILL
HEREFORD
CHERRY HILL CAMP
CAPLER CAMP
OLDBURY CAMP
CHASE WOOD CAMP
RIVER WYE
10 km
6 mi
N
Mercator

BRITISH CAMP, HEREFORDSHIRE BEACON

British Camp is one of the finest and most spectacular multivallate contour hillforts in the country. It is located on the high ridge of the Malvern Hills, standing at 338m above the Severn Valley to the east and the River Leadon to the west. The hillfort's snaking ramparts encompass the hill of Herefordshire Beacon itself and the summit to the south called Millennium Hill. The location of the hillfort is strategic, sitting above the primary pass through the Malvern Hills during ancient times at Wynds Point.

Wheeler (1953) suggested four phases of construction.

1: Initially in the late Bronze/early Iron Age, 3ha were enclosed by a slight bank and a ditch, which used the artificially steepened scarp slope.

2: During the middle Iron Age, the enclosure was enlarged by four times to a footprint of 13.5ha, with a bank and a deep ditch running along the 305m contour line with four overlapping entrances.

3: During the twelfth century after the Norman occupation, the ring work on the summit was constructed, comprising a rock-cut ditch with an internal bank.

4: The Shire Ditch or Red Earl's Dyke was constructed in 1287, following a boundary dispute between Gilbert De Clare, the Earl of Gloucester, and Thomas De Cantilupe, the Bishop of Hereford. The ditch runs north and south of British Camp along the ridge line and incorporates the counterscarp of the east ditch of the fort.

English Heritage carried out investigations in 1999 and 2000, and 118 hut platforms were identified to have been built in the phase two enlarged enclosure. The standard view of archaeologists is that these larger hillfort enclosures supported extensive permanent populations, which the hut platforms would tend to confirm. However, if these hillforts were permanently occupied, a number of problems arise. There are no internal track ways, and no evidence of domestic refuse or any farm activities. Also there is little or no evidence of where the local population buried their dead. An alternative theory (M. Bowden) is that British Camp and nearby Midsummer Hill were used for special seasonal occasions such as religious and ritual events, markets and festivals. The hut platforms, he suggests, were used as temporary accommodation or as market stalls for the social gatherings taking place.

British Camp was abandoned around the year 48 AD, coinciding with the expansion of the Roman legions into the West Country of Britain. Local folklore suggests the British chieftain Caractacus made his last stand here, but there has been no evidence of any violent resistance found. The Roman historian Tacitus tells us that the site of the battle was close to the River Severn. My suggestion is that this battle took place at Welshbury Camp in the Forest of Dean, standing 2.5km from the Severn, where it is reputed the Dobunni tribe made their last stand against the Romans.

British Camp has been excavated once (F.G. Hilton Price 1879); he concentrated on the summit of Herefordshire Beacon. The items uncovered at the time were re-examined by archaeologists in 2010, but they found the items dated back to medieval times, apart from a section of a Roman jar dating to the second or third century AD.

Parking is off the A449 at paying car park for British Camp (what3words: them.health.irony). A café and hotel is opposite the car park. The walk is 2km, more if you walk a circuit of the ramparts; difficulty four. Landranger map 150. Map ref. NGR 759400.

MIDSUMMER HILL

South of British Camp and still on the ridge of the Malvern Hills is a univallate partial contour fort. It occupies two hills, Midsummer Hill and Hollybush Hill, standing at 284m, with an intervening valley containing a spring. Surrounded by steep and rugged slopes now heavily wooded, the fort has a complete circuit (apart from the southern section of Hollybush Hill which has been quarried away) comprising of a rubble-built bank and ditch with a small counterscarp bank enclosing an irregular area of 7ha. The defences have been made more imposing by the ditch being up to 11m below the steep slope and rampart as illustrated in the photograph below. The two

surviving entrances on Midsummer Hill are original; the north-facing entrance is oblique and in-turned, while the southern entrance is in-turned, creating a narrow corridor above the steep slope.

Excavations (Stanford 1981) revealed seventeen phases of construction between 470 BC and 30 AD. Small hut platforms numbering 483 cut into the hillside have been recorded; whether they are evidence of accommodation or storage huts, the archaeology has shown that the site was possibly heavily populated during its existence. There has been evidence of bronze and iron smelting with ore from the nearby Forest of Dean with the process's resultant slag deposits. Hughes (1924) discovered examples of linear tooled and stamped Malvernian pottery wares from the Iron Age period.

The name 'Midsummer Hill' lends itself to the same modern theory as for British Camp (M Bowden) of the site being used for seasonal and occasional religious gatherings of peoples and not permanent occupation. If this was the case, the spring found between the two hills could have been of ritual significance. This may have been the case. I suggest in times of strife, hillforts, including Midsummer Hill and British Camp, amongst others, offered a place of refuge and resistance for the local population. Midsummer Hill was abandoned in 48 AD; evidence shows it was destroyed by fire, yet again coinciding with the advance of the Roman legions. Even though we have seen that these hillforts are impressive, they all succumbed to the Roman's superior siege tactics.

Parking is as for British Camp if you want a longer walk to visit both hillforts. Walk length 7km; difficulty four. For a shorter walk to just visit Midsummer Hill, park at Hollybush (what3words: clays.masks.mixer). Walk length 1.5km; difficulty four. Landranger map 150. Map ref. NGR 761375.

CREDENHILL CAMP

Unfortunately, owing to its close proximity to the British Army garrison in Credenhill famously named Stirling Lines and home to the headquarters of the 22 Special Air Service Regiment, there are no aerial photographs available of the hillfort due to drone flying restrictions. The hill which overlooks the garrison is open to the public, so I have taken photographs while walking the earthworks, but regrettably, though they illustrate the significant scale of the defences, they cannot show the size and extent of the camp.

On a densely wooded knoll standing at 210m above and dominating a major bend in the River Wye is the bivallate contour hillfort of Credenhill Camp. Enclosing almost 20ha it is one of the largest hillforts in Britain after Ham Hill, Somerset and Maiden Castle, Dorset, and twice as large as any other hillfort in Herefordshire. Roughly oval in shape, the earthworks have double concentric ramparts with a medial ditch and are substantial, with the inner bank 9m in height and the outer bank which stands at 4m. The southern rampart scarps the already steep natural slope to increase the monumentality of the defences, with a berm that runs along the base of the scarp. There are two entrances to the south-east and east, both with in-turns providing long approach passages with possible guard chambers.

A photograph on the next page was taken from inside the inner ditch, illustrating the scale of the ramparts.

Excavations (Stanford 1963) revealed post holes for many structures, including dwellings, timber granaries and storage pits. Stanford was the first to publish a discussion of a defended settlement where buildings appear to be regularly spaced rectangular structures, and further suggested that the site may have held up to 4000 people and could have been the political capital of the northern region of the Dobunni tribe. There is evidence of Bronze Age occupation of the hill, with pottery sherds uncovered that pre-date the estimated construction of the later Iron Age Camp at around 390 BC. Under the Roman Governor Publius Ostorius Scapula, the Roman legions following the defeat of the Dobunni in the Malvern Hills advanced westwards into the rolling hills of modern-day Herefordshire, ultimately reaching the regional capital of Credenhill. There has been no evidence found of burnt material or artefacts indicating that a battle took place at the site, but this does not mean resistance didn't take place in or around the area. Possibly after seeing what had occurred at previous sieges, a surrender was negotiated, and as Roman rule allowed, this regional hub became a client kingdom and another tax- and goods-producing area within the empire. The Romans used the site as a military depot until around 60 AD. Romano-British pottery was identified by Stanford, which may date from this period of military occupation. However, after the pacification of the region and the establishment of the town of Magnis (near modern-day Kenchester)—a couple of miles south of Credenhill and located on the strategically important Roman road of 'Watling Street' which ran south from Isca Silurium (Caerleon) north to Viroconium (Wroxeter)—the site of Credenhill was abandoned. In later times, the hill was used as a medieval deer park.

Credenhill Park Wood was purchased in 2002 by the Woodland Trust, which continues to manage and conserve the area. In the 1960s, the whole site was planted with conifers, but since 2008-2009, when the whole northern half of the site was cleared of woodland, there has been continuous work undertaken to thin the conifers that are shading out many important native trees, flora and fauna, and restore the ancient semi-natural woodland to its former glory.

Parking is at Credenhill Woods car park (what3words: tastes.surfer.guess). The walk that leads up from the car park is 4.3km in length; difficulty two. Landranger map 148. Map ref. NGR 451445.

SUTTON WALLS HILLFORT

On a low prominent hill overlooking the River Lugg floodplain is the univallate partial contour hillfort of Sutton Walls. The structure has an elongated shape running east to west, with the single bank and ditch following the 100m contour line around a complete circuit of the hill. The bank is now eroded to form a steep scarp with a terrace at its foot; now, the existing footpath around the feature. Dame Kathleen Kenyon excavated between 1948 and 1951 and suggests the original rampart would have stood up to 15m above a substantial V-shaped ditch some 32m wide. The ditch has been in-filled, but the size and scale of the rampart can still be appreciated as illustrated in the

section Ramparts, Walls and Ditches. The original entrances to the east and west have been damaged, but were formally in-turned with passageways; the current gaps to the north and south are modern. There is evidence that the fort was strengthened around the year AD 25, when a wooden palisade was added to the top of the rampart for the entire perimeter.

Excavations over several years, including the Time Team Project in 2000, revealed evidence of settlement in this area since Neolithic times through to the Iron Age, Romano-British and Saxon periods. Finds include Iron Age and Romano-British pottery, loom weights, spindle whorls and cheek pieces for bridles, showing us that this location was supporting a thriving community. A large iron anvil was discovered at Sutton Walls, and apparently this is one of the largest pre-Roman cast iron objects ever found in Britain.

Sutton Walls is linked to the site of a palace belonging to King Offa, the eighth-century Mercian King of Offa's Dyke fame, which, according to the Saxon Chronicle, tells us that it was a scene to a royal murder. In 794, Ethelbert, an East Anglian King betrothed to a daughter of Offa, had travelled to Sutton Walls for the wedding. He was taken captive and subsequently murdered and decapitated. Kenyon, during her extensive work, had excavated 24 skeletons from what was the ditch outside the western entrance, some of which had been decapitated and had arrow wounds. The initial theory was that they were local warriors unceremoniously dumped there following the attack on Sutton Walls by the legions of Publius Ostorius Scapula around 48 AD. Archaeologists are now theorising that these victims may have been King Ethelbert's East Anglian entourage, murdered along with him in 794.

Sadly the site has been mistreated over the years. The interior of the fort has been quarried, and in the 1960s and 70s was used as a landfill site, complete with toxic liquid lagoons. Sutton Walls was described in Michael Woods 'In Search of The Dark Ages' TV program during the King Offa episode as 'the worst example of archaeological conservation in Britain'. However, The Sutton Walls Conservation Group which was set up in 2017 to help manage and conserve the site has done a fantastic job in returning the site to a natural landscape. From the aerial photographs taken in 2022, there is very little or no evidence of the earlier environmental damage that had occurred in the interior of the fort.

Parking is on the street in the village of Sutton St Michael (what3words: himself.boasts.tins) opposite the bridleway that leads up to the fort. Walk length is 3.5km; difficulty two. Landranger map 149. Map ref. NGR 525464.

CROFT AMBREY

Sited on the summit of Yatton Hill at an elevation of 295m, above the wooded slopes leading down to a significant bend of the River Lugg, is the multivallate partial contour fort of Croft Ambrey. Roughly D-shaped, with steep slopes to the east, west and north, and moderate to the south, it comprises a complete circuit of three banks and ditches. Following excavations of the gate, the interior and the annexe (Stanford 1960-1966), there are suggestions of a phased construction and seven periods of occupation between 450 BC and 49 AD.

Initially a rampart, later removed with a ditch which is still visible enclosed an area of 2.2ha, within this area evidence was found of four poster dwellings or grain storage buildings. Around 390 BC, this initial bank was

levelled and the enclosure increased to 4ha; this extension is visible as an inner rampart and two outer banks and ditches. Later, an annexe was added to the south, which is defined by two weak banks and ditches, increasing the footprint to 8.4ha. The original two main entrances are found at the north-east corner, where the approach is protected by a turning of the two inner ramparts on the edge of a steep slope. The entrance found in the south-west is a complex one, where the approach is throughout works of the inner rampart with a hollow way and a narrow path leading to the interior.

In the second century AD, a mound was constructed within the southern annexe; suggestions were that this may have been a place of social gathering, perhaps a Romano-British temple or sacrificial shrine. Excavations by Stanford confirmed the mound was late Roman, but built on an earlier Roman terrace with evidence of animal sacrifice. A wide range of excavated finds lead to the fact that this location was a thriving Iron Age centre supporting an estimated population of between 500 and 900

people. The finds include Malvernian pottery, furnace lining, ore and slag, clay and limestone loom weights and a selection of iron tools including blades, sickles, nails and a spade. Within the interior of the fort are up to five pillow mounds; as we have seen in other locations, the earthworks provide a perfect adapted location for a medieval rabbit warren. The fort appears to have been abandoned around 48 AD; with evidence of burnt material, this ties in with the continuing campaign by Governor Publius Ostorius Scapula to subjugate the hillforts and peoples of modern-day Herefordshire.

The grounds on which Croft Ambrey hillfort stands is owned by the National Trust. A visit includes entry to Croft Castle, an on-site café and extensive grounds for walking and exploring (what3words: angers.rooks. poorly). The walk taking in the hillfort and grounds is about 5km; difficulty three. Landranger map 137. Map ref. NGR 444668.

WAPLEY CAMP

Wapley Camp occupies the western end of the summit of Wapley Hill. With an elevation of 320m, it is a largely isolated multivallate contour hillfort that overlooks the river valleys of the Lugg to the north and the Arrow to the south. From the valleys below, the defences look massive, with the banks running east to west; triangular in shape, the fort encloses 5.4ha. The earthworks vary in complexity on each side of the camp. Facing the north-east is a system of five ramparts standing between 2–6m in height, the innermost bank being the strongest. The three inner ramparts have two medial ditches: a berm between 4m and 5m and an outer ditch completing the defences. The southern-facing defences have four ramparts, all with medial ditches.

shaft/well which was excavated in the mid-twentieth century and is now fenced off and topped with a concrete lid. Legend says that Owain Glendwr

the Welsh Prince and rebel leader used Wapley Camp as a base during his campaign for Welsh independence against the English in the early fifteenth century. Pillow mounds are in evidence within the interior of the camp, again showing adapted medieval use of the earthworks for rabbit farming. A section of the wood is locally called 'the Warren' and the house located just south of the earthworks is called 'Warren House'.

Apart from the northern-facing rampart and slope which is part of a commercial conifer plantation, the camp is under Forestry Commission management. Since 2004, there has been continuous work to carry out scrub and bracken clearance, including conifer removal.

Car parking is found to the south-east of Wapley Camp, just off the road (what3words: detection.wobbling.elbowing). The walk is 3.8km; difficulty two. Landranger map 137. Map ref. NGR 345624.

BURFA BANK

Burfa Bank is a large elongated multivallate contour hillfort occupying the summit of an isolated hill with an elevation of 313m, which overlooks the Hindwell Brook Valley to the south and the Welsh border, which follows the Offa's Dyke Path around the western base of the hill. Steep, heavily wooded slopes, including conifer plantations, surround the hillfort and have badly damaged the earthworks; however, the summit has been partially cleared and consists of areas of grass and scrub.

The earthworks enclose an area of 5.6ha, measuring 700m by 230m, and in the north consist of two ramparts standing up to 3.5m in height with an outer deep ditch 6m below the top of the rampart. The south and south-east quadrant comprises a single bank 1.5m high with an outer ditch

0.9m deep, while the south-west has two banks along with an intermittent counterscarp along sections of the circuit. The original main entrance is located on the northern western rampart, and is complex, with overlapping banks providing a funnelled effect approach to the interior of the fort.

The photographs here show the elongated summit of Burfa Bank looking south and the main entrance located on the north-western rampart.

The car park is located at the western base of the hill, just off the B 4362 (what3words: september.faded.warriors). The walk is a circuit of 3km; difficulty three. Landranger map 137. Map ref. NGR 285610.

CAPLER CAMP, WOLDBURY CAMP

Strategically sited on a steeply sloping spur at an elevation of 182m, overlooking a major bend of the River Wye, is the multivallate hillfort of Capler Camp. Occupying the long, narrow summit of the hill, the structure measures 620m by 150m. The scarp to the west is almost a sheer drop down to the river below; the northern-facing slope is steep, providing natural defence, whereas the southern slope is moderate. The western half of the 4.6ha enclosed area is heavily

wooded, including conifer plantations; the east is more open and the earthworks are plainly visible.

The south-facing side of Capler Camp is strategically weaker, having the shallower slopes that lead up to two banks which stand up to 4m in height, and ditches which measure 5m wide. On the south-west quadrant, there are three banks and a second ditch with a prominent counterscarp which contours around to the north-west corner. The north- and west-facing scarps are steep and provide natural protection, and are defended by a ditch only, which has a prominent counterscarp which contours around the west to the north-west corner. A track runs from the ditch in the north-west corner along the north-facing scarp which possibly masks or utilizes the counterscarp or berm. There are two entrances: one to the south, which is possibly modern; the other facing east is original and has in-turned ramparts. Situated south of this entrance is a sub-circular mound approximately 30m in diameter. Suggestions are that this may have been a

barbican protecting the entrance; however, there is no evidence to support this.

The hillfort is also known as 'Woldbury Camp'; tradition has it that the camp was a burial site for a local British chieftain. Excavations (Jack, Hayter 1925) found evidence of metal working and later Roman influence, including a coin from the reign of the Roman Empress Lucilla (164-169 AD) which currently resides in Hereford Museum along with fourth-century Romano-British pottery.

There is a small car park (what3words: kilts.prelude.supposes) which is located opposite the bridleway leading up to Capler Camp. The walk is 3km; difficulty two. Landranger map 149. Map ref. NGR 593329.

OTHER HILLFORTS OF HEREFORDSHIRE

There are numerous other hillforts located in Herefordshire not covered in this book, but we will concern ourselves here with three that border the River Wye which lend themselves to be potential frontier settlements. The first is Chase Wood Camp (photographed below), situated on a prominent, isolated hill overlooking the River Wye and the town of Ross on Wye. Steep slopes surround this partial contour fort, which stands at an elevation of 203m, is oval-

shaped and encloses an area of 10.8ha. The more moderate slopes to the south are topped by a rampart 2m in height, while to the west the defences unusually are located 40m downslope from the interior and consist of a berm at the base of the scarp, a ditch and a counterscarp. Parking is at the Town and Country Trail car park, Ferndown Road, Ross on Wye (what3words: hides.delighted.foil). The walk is 3.6km in length, difficulty four. Landranger map 149. Map ref. NGR 602223.

Cherry Hill Camp sits atop a prominent spur with an elevation of 140m, overlooking the town of Fownhope and the River Wye. Steep slopes surround the remains of this multivallate hillfort, which is now heavily wooded and this has led to root damage and erosion of the ramparts and ditches. Parking is on Fownhope sports field car park next to the pavilion (what3words: brain.simulator.briefing). The walk is 2.2km in length; difficulty 4. Landranger map 149. Map ref. NGR 577352.

Oldbury (photographed above) is a large oval univallate contour hillfort located on Ridge Hill near Much Marcle and a few kilometres east of a major bend of the River Wye. Partly wooded, with the interior given over to arable farming, the ramparts followed the contours of the ridge and are still visible on the northern arc of the fort. The ramparts then use the top of the ridge line running south, but have largely been damaged by agriculture on the southern and eastern sides. On-road parking is available (what3words: cheer.marinated.league). You can walk around the inside perimeter of the fort, with some great views of the rolling Herefordshire countryside; the walk is 2.2km; difficulty two. Landranger map 149. Map ref. NGR 632326.

CONCLUSION

The subject matter of this book is a hot topic in a number of ways, the first being the various views held on the use hillforts. Were these structures defensive military strongholds or livestock enclosures, were they occupied or unoccupied. The span of time from when these earthworks were initially constructed some as far back as the Bronze Age would mean they had been in existence for a 1000 years or more before the Claudian Roman invasion took place in 43 AD. These sites over the centuries may have had many phases of construction, use and occupation. As we have seen there are examples of sites such as Croft Ambrey, Herefordshire, having phases of expansion and renewal during its active period. Other sites were initially occupied then abandoned and subsequently reoccupied such as Crickley Hill, reasons as discussed may have been the political situation, climate change which could lead to problems such as plague, drought and the harvest failing. Initially many of these sites were defended enclosures for extended families and their livestock, but over time the population grew and settlements expanded into the larger hillfort enclosures we see today. Other settlements had Neolithic and Bronze Age history, showing us that the people of the Iron Age held their ancestors and ancient places of worship in esteem by incorporating causewayed enclosures and barrows within or near their earthworks. However, in the late Iron Age when society became increasingly hierarchical, status, power and wealth became ever important to dominant individuals altering the socio political situation. This lead to the development of the larger hillforts, and the strengthening of the defences of others, the strongmen showing their status in locations such as British Camp, Herefordshire and Liddington Castle, Wiltshire. The second potential controversy is my interpretation of the extent of the Dubonnic region which to many may seem ambitious and wholly unrealistic.

We will never know for sure how far the Dobunnic sphere of influence was but I have stated my case and I am sure the subject will continue to be hotly debated in the future and I welcome it.

As discussed earlier this list of hillforts visited in this book is not exhaustive for this region. Since writing this book I have visited another fifteen hillfort sites in West Country not included here. A majority of these are not as visual as the ones included in this book, the sites being heavily wooded or inaccessible to the public. However, they are all shown as earthworks, settlements or ancient monuments on the Ordnance Survey maps, go and explore and find them, they are out there. The list includes: in Gloucestershire, Shenberrow Camp, Beckbury Camp, Birdlip Camp, Salmonsbury. South Gloucestershire, Elberton Camp, Bury Hill near Winterborne. Wiltshire, Bincknoll Castle near Wroughton, Bury Camp near Colerne.

Hopefully now, after digesting the information supplied within this book, you, the reader, will have an increased knowledge of the history of the people and structure of Iron Age society, specifically the Dobunni Tribe, our ancient ancestors who constructed these impressive earthworks. Also, the reader will now have an insight into the development, construction and classifications of the different types of hillforts. Armed with this information, a trip to visit one of these sites should be more enlightening as one considers the landscape in question in a new and hopefully more enjoyable way. An important last thought to consider when walking around the ramparts, especially the larger structures, is that all of the work on these earthworks was carried out manually.

BIBLIOGRAPHY

M. Avery, *Hillfort Defences of Southern Britain, Vol I, II, III* (Bar Publishing, 1993).

M. Bowden, *The Middle Iron Age On The Marlborough Downs* (Oxbow Books, 2005).

S. Campbell, *Hill-Forts of the Cotswolds* (Amberley Publishing, 2016).

B. Cunliffe, *Iron Age Communities in Britain* (Routledge & Kegan Paul Ltd, Revised Edition 1978).

J. Dyer, *Hillforts of England & Wales* (Shire Publications, 2003).

G. Lock and I. Ralston. *Atlas of Hillforts of Britain and Ireland* (2017). Available at: hillforts.arch.ox.ac.uk

T. Moore, *Iron Age Societies in the Severn-Cotswolds: Developing Narratives of Social and Landscape Change* (BAR, British Series, 2006).

S. J. Yeates, *The Tribe of Witches: The Religion of the Dobunni and Hwicce* (Oxbow Books Ltd, 2008).